2041328

AF709193

30°°

DE HAGNIAE HEREDITATE

MNEMOSYNE

BIBLIOTHECA CLASSICA BATAVA

COLLEGERUNT

W. DEN BOER • W. J. VERDENIUS • R. E. H. WESTENDORP BOERMA

BIBLIOTHECAE FASCICULOS EDENDOS CURAVIT

W. J. VERDENIUS, HOMERUSLAAN 53, ZEIST

SUPPLEMENTUM QUADRAGESIMUM QUARTUM

WESLEY E. THOMPSON

DE HAGNIAE HEREDITATE

LUGDUNI BATAVORUM E. J. BRILL MCMLXXVI

DE HAGNIAE HEREDITATE

AN ATHENIAN INHERITANCE CASE

BY

WESLEY E. THOMPSON

LUGDUNI BATAVORUM E. J. BRILL MCMLXXVI

ISBN 90 04 04757 3

PRINTED IN THE NETHERLANDS

TO MY MOTHER

CONTENTS

PREFACE

The great Athenian advocates, Lysias, Isaeus, and Demosthenes, invariably present a one-sided interpretation of the case at hand, quite naturally putting their client's version in the most favorable light and distorting their opponent's reply. Seldom do we have an opportunity to hear the other side, and seldom do we know the outcome of the trial. A notable exception is the struggle for control of the estate of a man named Hagnias, where we can hear both sides of the story—or, I should say, two sides of the story, for at least five separate claims to this inheritance were entered in several trials over a long period of time. We also know the verdict in most of these trials, which ought to help us evaluate the issues and the work of the speech writers.

Strangely enough, however, interpreters have generally refused to accept the validity of the verdicts. Partly this is due to the reputation of one of the writers, Isaeus, of whom the ancient literary critic Dionysius of Halicarnassus says, "Not even if he tells the truth, will the reader heed him without suspicion." (Cf. his *Isaeus*, § 16.) So it is with modern writers, especially Wyse in his standard commentary on Isaeus. Moreover, Isaeus represents Hagnias' second cousin against a woman, Phylomache, who claimed to be his first cousin once removed. Since most scholars interpret the Athenian inheritance law to favor this relationship but to exclude second cousins from consideration, they have treated Isaeus as the devil's advocate, who sought by *suppressio veri* and *innuendo* to make the Unjust Logos appear superior to the Just.

On the other hand, Phylomache's representative, her husband Sositheos, is regarded as an innocent bungler, who failed to establish the case which he rightfully had in law. A few scholars, however, have seen that we must rely on the ability of the Athenian courts which repeatedly upheld Isaeus' side. Sositheos' failure is due less to ineptitude than to the weakness of his position. While most interpreters have seen here a clear-cut case of a good legal basis against a false one, what is really at stake for Sositheos' side is a question of fact, not one of law. Yes, a first cousin once removed outranked a second cousin, but was Phylomache what she claimed to be? For her opponents alleged that her grandmother was not actually related to Hagnias, thereby breaking the link between Phylomache and the *de cuius*. That is the charge which Sositheos had to refute before he could win the prize. He apparently failed to do so.

It should be obvious that, if Isaeus was in the right and his opponents in the wrong, we must adopt an entirely different attitude toward his handling of the case. Instead of condemning (or admiring) his sleight of hand, we can applaud the lucidity of his straight-forward presentation of the issues. Likewise, instead of wondering why Sositheos or his speech writer failed to point out and hammer home the blatant fraud which Isaeus perpetrated, we can see more clearly how he sought to emphasize the strong points of his case and to bolster his arguments on the crucial point, the relationship between Hagnias and Phylomache's grandmother.

Therefore, I have written a running commentary on their speeches (Isaeus 11 and Ps.-Dem. 43) from this heterodox standpoint, attempting some appreciation of both writers' problems and skills, discussing doubtful points of law whenever necessary, and trying to correct Wyse's malicious treatment of Isaeus and his client. The work is intended mainly for people interested in techniques of persuasion and does not require a knowledge of Greek for its use.

MAIN PARTICIPANTS

Hagnias, whose estate is in question
Glaukos and Glaukon, his half-brothers
the mother of these three

Theopompos, Isaeus' client and holder of Hagnias' estate
Makartatos, his son and successor to Hagnias' estate
the elder Makartatos, Theopompos' brother-in-law

Stratokles, Theopompos' brother
his son, Theopompos' ward
his other guardian, who is suing Theopompos on the boy's behalf

Sositheos, the speaker of Ps.-Dem. 43 against Makartatos
Phylomache II, his wife
Euboulides II, her father
Euboulides III, the claimant in Ps.-Dem. 43, Sositheos' son, adopted as the son of Euboulides II

Hagnias I, the grandfather of the *de cuius*
Phylomache I, allegedly his daughter and the mother of Euboulides II, thus the link between the *de cuius* and the line of Euboulides
Bouselos, the fountainhead of this entire family

MAIN EVENTS

c. 396	Hagnias dies, leaving a will adopting his niece
c. 385	the niece dies, and Glaukon takes control of the estate
361/0	Phylomache II breaks the will and wins the estate
c. 360	Theopompos wins the estate from her
soon after	Isaeus 11: he defends himself against his ward
c. 350	Makartatos succeeds Theopompos on his death
c. 345	Ps.-Dem. 43: Sositheos tries to wrest the estate from him

PARTIAL STEMMA

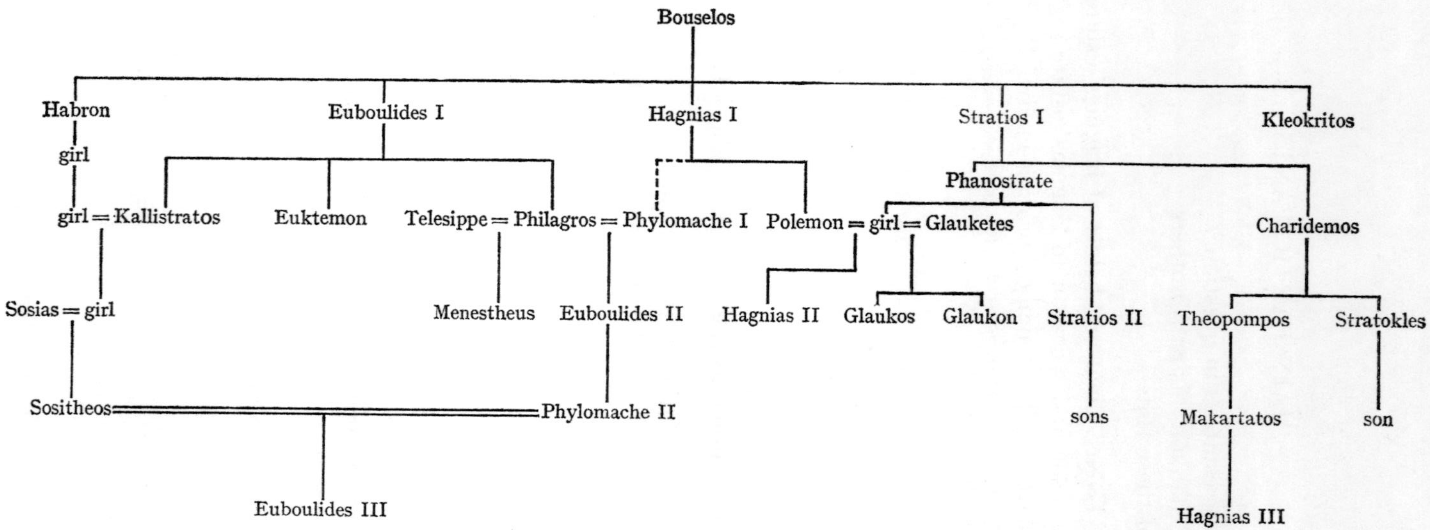

By alloting a half-generation to four of the girls in this stemma we can illustrate the main relationships among the cousins in this family and also observe the effect of the early marriage of females.

IMPORTANT ABBREVIATIONS

Broadbent	Molly Broadbent, *Studies in Greek Genealogy* (Leiden, 1968)
Harrison	A. R. W. Harrison, *The Law of Athens* (Oxford, 1968-1971)
Jebb	R. C. Jebb, *Selections from the Attic Orators* (London, 1888): all citations from this work are *ad. loc.*
Wyse	William Wyse, *The Speeches of Isaeus* (Cambridge, 1904): again, all citations are *ad loc.* unless otherwise noted
ms.	the Cripps manuscript of Isaeus, the chief authority for the text

PART ONE

ISAEUS II: MAIN DIVISIONS OF THE SPEECH

§§		
1-6	Discussion of the inheritance law	
7-10	Narrative I	
11-14	Proof I: Theopompos alone is entitled to the inheritance	
15-19	Narrative II	
	Proof II	
20-23	a.	Theopompos did not agree to share with Stratokles
24-26	b.	Theopompos did not agree to share with his ward
27-31	Re-rebuttal	
32-36	*Metalepsis*	
	Rebuttal: comparison of estates	
37-39	a.	the issue
40-43	b.	Stratokles' estate
44-50	c.	Theopompos' estate
lost	d.	his opponent's villainy
lost	e.	his own skilful management of his ward's estate
lost	Peroration	

THEOPOMPOS' SPEECH
(Isaeus 11)

1. Theopompos' fellow guardian, who represents their ward in this action, claims that Theopompos and his brother Stratokles were entitled to equal shares of Hagnias' estate and that Stratokles' rights devolved on his son, the ward. In so arguing, he quoted only a portion of the law regulating the inheritance of one who died childless and intestate. As we learn from Sositheos' speech (51), this section went as follows: "if there are homopatric brothers, (they shall inherit), and if there are legitimate children of brothers, they shall have their father's portion." Certainly the Athenians recognized the principle of representation and division by *stirpes*. If a brother dies and is survived only by a second brother and the two sons of a third brother, the sons receive their father's share (1/4 of the estate each) and the remaining brother receives half. Theopompos' opponent tries to apply the principle to cousins: since Theopompos and Stratokles, as his second cousins, would each receive one half of Hagnias' estate, Stratokles' son should then receive his father's share. But Isaeus will correctly show that the principle of representation has its limits and that the line of succession stops at second cousins, such as Theopompos and Stratokles, and does not include their offspring.

Γένος is normally translated "degree". A degree in English law is a generation, and relationship is computed in generations (degrees) distant from the deceased, reckoned lineally, upwards and downwards. Thus a son and the father of the deceased are in the first degree, and a grandson and brother are in the second. (The brother is related through the father and not directly.) An uncle and a nephew are both in the third degree in the English system, but a nephew outranks an uncle in the Attic, which follows a different principle, reckoning kinship from a common ancestor. In this system the descendants of a nearer ancestor outrank the offspring of a farther ancestor. An uncle is descended from the deceased's grandfather, but a nephew is descended from the deceased's father and so is closer. In view of the different approaches to reckoning, "degree" is inadequate as a translation of γένος, and Wyse therefore suggests "stock". Unfortunately, however, in English law the "stock" is the common ancestor of collateral kin.[1] For want of a better alternative I translate, "inheritance class," since Theopompos names the heirs in three groups, brothers, sisters, and cousins (along with their respective offspring). It should be noted that Theopompos does not suggest that all members of a group were equally entitled to inherit, and certainly a first cousin outranked a second cousin. (Γένος in the text of our ms. is predicate: "this is, as an inheritance class, nearest the deceased." I see no reason to follow modern editors who add the definite article τό, altering the meaning to "this inheritance class is nearest the deceased" or "this is the inheritance class nearest the deceased.")

Since most Greek forensic speeches begin with a fairly complex or even ornate address to the jury, some scholars have supposed that Theopompos must have used the same approach and that his introduction has been omitted in the ms. Schömann, I think, is closer to the truth in suggesting that this abrupt beginning which we have was Isaeus' way of getting the jury's attention: since they were expecting the usual formal introduction, they responded favorably when Theopompos got right down to business.[2] This explanation accords well with my conception of Theopompos' objective. Since on legal grounds he had every right to possess Hagnias' estate, and his opponent had no standing at all, Theopompos wanted to present that legal position as simply and lucidly as possible, and he had no need to prevaricate or engage in rhetorical flourishes. Since his case is based on the law, he begins with the law. (Incidentally, although he says, "I read you the law," presumably it was the court clerk who actually did so.)

2. The law granted the right of succession up to and including "the offspring of cousins," ἀνεψιῶν παίδων. Theopompos' case depends on the meaning of this term. Most scholars simply assume that it means "sons of the deceased's cousins" (i.e., his first cousins once removed). But linguistically there is another way of understanding the phrase. The sons of a man are brothers (ἀδελφοί). *Their* sons are cousins (ἀνεψιοί). *Their* sons are second cousins,

[1] Sir William Blackstone, *Commentaries on the Laws of England* 2.14, *passim*.

[2] G. F. Schömann, *Isaei Orationes XI cum aliquot Deperditarum Fragmentis* (Greifswald, 1831), 454. Isaeus 3 also begins without the usual formal introduction, and the literary critic Dionysius of Halicarnassus (*Isaeus* 15) cites another speech, now lost, in which Isaeus discusses the meaning of the inheritance law before proceeding to his narrative.

"offspring of cousins," ἀνεψιῶν παῖδες.[3] What recommends this interpretation is the fact that Theopompos won the estate in the first place and defended it successfully in two subsequent trials (the one at hand and a defense against a charge of perjury[4]). In his first trial he ousted Phylomache from possession of the estate by proving to the satisfaction of the jury that her grandmother was not the lawful daughter of Hagnias' grandfather. This destroyed the basis for Phylomache's claim to the estate, but by itself this success would not win Hagnias' property for Theopompos. He had to defeat other challengers. If the right to inherit was limited to first cousins once removed and did not extend to second cousins, then once Phylomache had been discredited, the estate would revert to Hagnias' maternal relatives. But Theopompos defeated them too. Unless Athenian juries were so stupid that on three separate occasions they held for an imposter, ἀνεψιῶν παίδων in the inheritance law must mean "second cousins." If Theopompos had blatantly won in defiance of the law, it would have presented Sositheos a golden opportunity to vilify him in his turn (Ps.-Dem. 43), but Sositheos does not undertake to show what modern interpreters think so obvious, that Theopompos had no legal standing. The reason is, I submit, that on the legal plane Theopompos' case was solidly grounded. It is the facts that were in dispute, and that is what Sositheos concentrates on, calling witnesses to prove that Phylomache's grandmother was actually the lawful child of Hagnias' grandfather. One final consideration ought to show that Theopompos had a legal right to Hagnias' estate. Athenian legal procedure permitted someone with a better claim to file a challenge even after an estate had been adjudicated. That is how Theopompos took it away from Phylomache, and how Sositheos attempted to take it back from Theopompos' son. If maternal relatives outranked second cousins, as most critics would have us believe, the way was open for Hagnias' maternal first cousins to oust Theopompos.

---

[3] Cf. John C. Miles, "The Attic Law of Intestate Succession," Hermathena 75 (1950), 69-77. A German translation of this article appears in *Zur griechischen Rechtsgeschichte*, ed. Erich Berneker (Darmstadt, 1968), 655-665.

[4] Theopompos says in section 45 that perjury *trials* are pending, but acquittal in one would probably cause the prosecution to abandon the others. If none of the cases was brought to trial, that would simply be further evidence that Theopompos had a strong position. It is also very likely that Makartatos defeated Sositheos in the renewal of the struggle; cf. Part Two, *The verdict*.

They were the sons of Stratios, the brother of Hagnias' mother. But they did not do so (see sections 15-16).[5]

Sositheos quotes the Athenian inheritance law at section 51, but unluckily the mss. have a lacuna there. We may paraphrase the text as follows: "Whoever dies intestate, if he leaves daughters (the estate goes) with them. Otherwise the following are to have control of his possessions. If there are homopatric brothers, (they shall inherit), and if there are legitimate children of brothers, they shall have their father's portion. But if there are no brothers or children of brothers . . . (lacuna) . . . from them shall receive a portion on the same terms. And males and the sons of males are to prevail, if they are of the same (ancestors) even if they are further removed in kinship. But if there is no one on the father's side within the degree of second cousin, those on the man's mother's side are to have control according to the same terms. But if there is no one within this rank on either side, the nearest relative on the father's side is to have control. But an illegitimate son or daughter shall have no right of succession to religious or temporal privileges, beginning with the archonship of Eukleides" (403/2). To overcome the textual problem here scholars have generally sought out the various people eligible to inherit and inserted their titles in the lacuna. This results in such texts as "<homopatric sisters and the offspring> from them shall receive a portion" or "<homopatric sisters and their children are to have a share, but if there are no sisters or their children, the uncles and aunts and the offspring> from them shall receive a portion." But this is probably the wrong way of going about it. Since Theopompos says that the law was more concise than his explanation of it, it seems probable that the law itself did not name everyone who was entitled to inherit but left it up to the jury to apply general principles to specific instances. (The law goes back to Solon, who regularly adopted this technique.)[6] I do not think that we can recover the original text.[7]

Whatever the true text here, we must reject Wyse's criticism of

---

[5] A. R. W. Harrison also holds that the crucial phrase ἀνεψιῶν παῖδες means second cousins, but he derives this meaning by taking ἀνεψιῶν as first cousins once removed, a meaning attested only at Sos. 41 and 49; cf. his "A Problem in the Rules of Intestate Succession at Athens," C. R. 61 (1947), 41-43.

[6] Cf. Plutarch *Solon* 18.

[7] For a different version cf. Eberhard Ruschenbusch, ΣΟΛΩΝΟΣ ΝΟΜΟΙ (Historia, Einzelschrift 9, Wiesbaden, 1966), 87-88 (F 50b).

Isaeus' paraphrase of the law: "If after mentioning brothers and sisters of the deceased on the father's side the law went on to specify brothers and sisters of the father of the deceased with their children, what motive had Isaeus for describing the '3rd stock' as 'cousins and children of cousins'? The answer is simple. Here, as in § 11. 5, he was afraid of injuring his case. Theopompus and Stratocles were second cousins of the deceased . . . while their rival Phylomache II claimed to be the granddaughter of Phylomache I, full sister of Polemon father of Hagnias II. These are facts which Isaeus wished to keep out of sight." However, since Theopompos has already convinced one jury that Phylomache II was not actually a first cousin once removed to Hagnias, as she claimed, he should have no hesitation in admitting that this rank could inherit. And indeed when he says that the law assigns the right of inheritance to cousins up to second cousins, he certainly includes first cousins once removed. Moreover, Phylomache's own representative, Sositheos, constantly harps on the phrase ἀνεψιοῦ παῖς (cousin's child) to justify his own position and never says a word about the right of an uncle to inherit. Perhaps the inheritance law did specifically mention uncles and aunts, but since neither was involved in the case, there was no reason for Theopompos or Sositheos to raise the point.

Keeping the reading of the ms., Jebb interprets Isaeus' meaning as, "Failing these also, the law reverts to the direct line [εἰς τὸ γένος, the *direct* lineage on the *maternal* side as opp. to collateral kinship on the paternal]." However, this abrupt change in meaning for γένος, from "inheritance class" to "direct lineage" is too harsh for me, so I prefer the modern editor's excision of εἰς. Thus, "if this class fails, then the law reverts . . ."

3. When Theopompos expands on the law, I think that he does so to clarify it and not to deceive the jury about some crucial point of wording. In any event, although the law provides that in the absence of paternal or maternal second cousins (or anyone closer) the nearest paternal relative shall inherit, Theopompos regularly ignores this remote possibility and always refers to second cousins and closer kin as in the line of succession (*anchisteia*) or related to the deceased (προσήκοντες), while anyone else is always outside the *anchisteia* and not related. In this case, though, rather than saying that the boy is outside the line of succession, Theopompos says that he is outside the kinship. Jebb explains that "'outside the kinship',

= outside of *that* kinship which the law recognizes as constituting ἀγχιστεία." That seems quite a lot for the hearer to supply. I think that this is one of several times that Isaeus uses a technical term loosely.[8] Here he is probably seeking variation and in order to avoid saying, "line of succession," again substitutes "kinship".

Since the boy was a second cousin once removed to Hagnias, his relationship was not one of those included within the group of cousins up to ἀνεψιῶν παίδων (second cousins). Theopompos was on safe ground in challenging his opponent to specify the boy's connection with the deceased and in offering to yield the half of the estate which his opponent was claiming for their ward, as the successor to Stratokles. The orators regularly challenge their adversaries to prove something but rarely promise them a reward for doing so.[9]

4. Although a party to a suit could not testify in his own behalf, he could be required to answer questions put by his opponent. In three speeches of Lysias we have what purports to be an exchange between interrogator and respondent,[10] but we are entitled to suspect that Lysias has taken the opportunity of editing his speeches to defang any clever answer his opponent may have given and to sharpen up his own examination. In the present case it looks as though Theopompos could speak his set piece no matter what his fellow guardian said in reply to his questions.

5. Theopompos apparently asks whether the boy was (born) of a cousin, but this is no indication that the line of succession ended with first cousins once removed. Surely Isaeus is too wily to admit that, even if true. By "(born) of a cousin" he means ἀνεψιοῦ παῖς, "son of a cousin." 'Ανεψιῶν παῖδες was a rarely used technical term, and it was difficult to form the singular of the word.[11] While it is easy to say that you and I are "sons of cousins," i.e., second cousins, it is not so obvious how to say that I am your second cousin. Is it "son of cousin" or "son of cousins"? Isaeus opts for the former.

[8] Wyse notes that the same laxity can be found at Plato *Laws* 925B. Other instances of imprecision in this speech include the use of ἀνεψιαδῶν to mean "second cousins" at 12, μίσθωσιν τῶν ἐκείνου χρημάτων at 34 instead of the regular expression μίσθωσιν οἴκου, and γραφή for εἰσαγγελία at 31 and 35. Cf. also Jean-Marc Denommé, *Recherches sur la langue et le style d'Isée* (Hildesheim, 1974), 38-39.

[9] Cf. § 34 and Ps.-Dem. 44.7-8.

[10] 12.25, 13.30-33, and 22.5.

[11] See the commentary on § 10.

In the subsequent trial Theopompos' son Makartatos reverses the argument (Sos. 60), saying that once the estate passed from Hagnias to Theopompos the crucial issue became a claimant's relationship to Theopompos and not to Hagnias. In the present instance Isaeus is correct to insist that the relationship to Hagnias is all-important. In doing so, however, he obscures his opponent's position, which is not that the boy is Theopompos' nephew and thus entitled to part of what he has. Rather the opponent is saying that as Stratokles' son the boy has a right to the share his father would have received, had he lived.

6. Isaeus' wording goes beyond the simple statement that Theopompos' opponent should swear an oath so that he might be believed and carries with good effect the implication that, if he were willing to swear, he would now be more believable than he actually is.[12] Interpreters of Attic law differ on the nature of the oath involved, what it should have covered, and when it should have been given. One view is that the opponent failed to specify the boy's relationship to Hagnias in the oath which he took at the preliminary hearing.[13] Another is that Theopompos demanded an oath during the trial itself.[14] It seems to me that both interpretations are too specific; Theopompos is talking in generalities, saying that any honest man would be willing to take an oath, without having a particular occasion in mind.

On the nature of these proceedings (*eisangelia*) see the commentary on section 31.

Actually, of course, Theopompos' opponent has made some sort of reply, has sworn some kind of oath, has read out a portion of the law, and needs no witnesses to establish the boy's kinship. Yet Isaeus ignores all this since he wants to finish this unit of the speech with a fine rhetorical display, combining anaphora, asyndeton, and chiasmus.[15] In his opening the orator has succeeded in

---

[12] This is true whether we accept or reject the particle ἄν which the ms. has. Normally it is not used in this construction, but the mss. at Plato *Laws* 959C also have ἄν, and I do not see why we should alter two passages to achieve a rigid uniformity of language.

[13] M. H. E. Meier, G. F. Schömann, J. H. Lipsius, *Der attische Process* (Berlin, 1883-1887), 825, n. 178.

[14] Justus H. Lipsius, *Das attische Recht und Rechtsverfahren* (Leipzig, 1905-1915), 833, n. 16.

[15] In the sentence, "he has given no answer . . . quoted no law," Isaeus uses the perfect and aorist tenses in chiastic sequence, and by reiterating the negative, he mingles repetition with variety. For a somewhat weaker combination of asyndeton cf. 8.29.

what he set out to do. He has disproved one of the two contentions which his adversary had advanced to justify the boy's claim to half the estate: the principle of representation does not secure Stratokles' portion for his son, since it does not operate past the rank of second cousin. The other contention, that Theopompos agreed to yield half of Hagnias' property, is taken up later (§§ 20-30), as Isaeus now turns from the negative to the positive.

7. Now, as is the custom in Athenian forensic speeches, Isaeus begins his narrative of the events leading up to the trial. In doing so, he alerts the jury to listen for two points: why Theopompos is entitled to Hagnias' estate and why his opponents are not. This latter point rests on showing that they are outside the *anchisteia*. One must bear in mind that, as Isaeus uses this term, it means kin up to (and including) second cousins. Even though a second cousin once removed could inherit, if no closer relative was alive, Isaeus simply does not entertain the possibility.

8. Sositheos (19) informs us that Bouselos had five sons, Hagnias, Euboulides, Stratios, Kleokritos, and Habron. Of the cousins mentioned by Isaeus, Hagnias was the son of Polemon, Euboulides the son of Philagros (both named for their paternal grandfather), and Theopompos and his brother were the sons of Charidemos and grandsons of Stratios. Because of his name most scholars assume that the younger Stratios was also his grandson. Sositheos says that the elder Stratios had another child besides Charidemos. At § 22 of his speech some of the mss. call this person Phanostratos, others Phanostrate, but at § 42 the mss. unequivocally name "Phanostrate the daughter of Stratios." This should mean that the younger Stratios was her son. That would account for his name but not for the fact that Isaeus says that his *father* is one of the cousins born from uncles. Consequently, I conclude that his father must be a son of Habron or a son of Kleokritos, who married his cousin Phanostrate.[16]

Since female second cousins ranked below males of the same degree, Theopompos does not need to mention them. Apparently there were no first cousins once removed still living. (Of course, Theopompos would not admit that Phylomache was one of them.) The depositions attached to Sositheos' speech (44-45) say that Euboulides had a half-brother named Menestheus, who refrained

[16] For other examples of this type of marriage cf. my article, "The Marriage of First Cousins in Athenian Society," Phoenix 21 (1967), 273-282.

from claiming Hagnias' estate. Since Philagros was his father, Menestheus like Theopompos was a second cousin to Hagnias. Why does Theopompos neglect him? Anyone who mistrusts the authenticity of the depositions will have a ready answer. But if they are genuine, Menestheus' refusal to contest Euboulides' claim shows that he recognized his brother's kinship to Hagnias through Phylomache I, and that would explain Theopompos' silence. Moreover, Menestheus must have been dead by the time Phylomache filed her claim, or the depositions would say that he yielded to her too. Therefore, he played no part in the episode which Theopompos is narrating.

Hagnias had two maternal half-brothers, Glaukon and Glaukos, whose father was apparently called Glauketes, and perhaps other siblings who are not mentioned in our speeches.[17] I prefer to accept the natural implication of the text that his niece was a maternal relative. If the girl were related to Hagnias through his father, she would be his next of kin (as a niece she would outrank Theopompos); if through his mother, she was not. Theopompos has no reason to lie about her relationship since she was dead and, in any event, he acknowledges the will. It also seems likely from his description that

[17] Remarriage was common at Athens, and we find many half-brothers and half-sisters mentioned in the surviving speeches; cf. my article, "Athenian Marriage Patterns: Remarriage," California Studies in Classical Antiquity 5 (1972), 211-225. Since the deposition at § 31 of Sositheos' speech shows that Glaukos and Glaukon were still alive in 361, Glauketes was apparently the second husband of Hagnias' mother. The known members of his family can be arranged in a (perhaps oversimplified) stemma along the following lines:

Glauketes

Glaukos — Glaukon — - - - Glaukippos

Glaukos: member of Boule, c. 370 (*I.G.* II^2 1742, lines 85-86; cf. Hesperia 16 [1947], 151)

Glaukos' son: Glauketes, participates in Pythian festival, c. 326 (*S.I.G.*^{3} 296, 297B; cf. Hesperia 30 [1961], 43-44)

Glaukippos' son: Glauketes, dies, c. 317 (*I.G.* II^2 6987/8)

A certain Glauketes of Oion was born in 389/8 and served as public arbitrator in 330/29; cf. D. M. Lewis, "Notes on Attic Inscriptions (II)," B. S. A. 50 (1955), 27-36. Glaukippos may have been a nephew of the first Glauketes rather than his son, nor is it certain that the Glaukos who served in the Boule was our man.

Glaukon is not her father. Thus she would be the daughter of Glaukos or some other member of this side of the family.

Sositheos gives prominence to Glaukon's brother, saying that "Glaukos of Oion and Glaukon his brother came forward with a false will," which Phylomache exposed in her first trial (4), and describing her opponents in the second as Theopompos, Glaukon, and Glaukos, "the one who was defeated before." (7) It is hard to see what either Theopompos or Sositheos could gain by lying about the identity of the (alleged) testamentary heir. Perhaps the truth, then, is that Glaukos intended to be his own father's heir and arranged for Glaukon to become Hagnias' heir. As a result, Sositheos would paint him as the villain of the piece.[18]

The author of the *Hellenica Oxyrhynchia* relates that c. 396 the Athenians "sent ambassadors to the King of Persia... ---krates, Hagnias, and Telesegoros, whom Pharax the former admiral seized and sent to the Spartans, and they killed them,"[19] while Harpokration in his *Lexicon* to the Ten Orators says (*s.v.*, Ἁγνίας), "Androtion in the fifth book of his *Atthis* and Philochoros say that he and his fellow ambassadors were seized and killed by the Spartans."

Rather than see his line expire, a childless Athenian might adopt a son (normally a close relative) who would then inherit his estate and assume the responsibilities of the family cult. (For a list of such adoptions cf. Louis Gernet, "La création du testament," R. E. G. 33 [1920], 140-141, or his *Droit et Société dans la Grèce ancienne* [Paris, 1955], 129.) Because of the legal and social disabilities of women it was rare to adopt a daughter. In fact, many men who had a daughter adopted her husband or her son. But there were times when a prospective son wished to remain as his natural father's heir. This is certainly true in the only other two instances in the orators when men adopted a daughter. One of them was Stratokles' brother-in-law, Theophon (§ 41), who presumably wanted to adopt his nearest relative or perhaps gratify his sister. In any event, since Stratokles had only one son, Theophon adopted one of his daughters. In the other case (Isaeus 7.9) a man wrote a will adopting his homometric sister and marrying her to

[18] It seems likely to me that Sositheos, representing his wife, actually proceeded against Glaukos rather than Glaukon, attacking him as the forger of the will.

[19] *Hellenica Oxyrhynchia*, ed. Vittorio Bartoletti (Leipzig, 1959), 7.

a member of one of the families which administered the Eleusinian cult of Demeter and Kore. The fiancé certainly did not want to break off his own family connection. In effect, the will functioned as a marriage contract. In Hagnias' case, though, it would have been possible for him to adopt one of his half-brothers, and we cannot say why he did not.[20] (Since Athenian law permitted a man to name an heir in case his own sons should die before reaching manhood [Ps.-Dem. 46.24], there is nothing unusual about the alleged selection of Glaukon as a contingent heir.)

This section of Isaeus' speech raises several difficult and important problems. First, does Theopompos assert that Hagnias adopted his niece while he was still alive, or does he say that Hagnias simply left a will adopting her upon his death? I favor the latter alternative. In the first place, Isaeus' wording here is very similar to the language he uses in his sixth speech to describe an adoption by will. Compare, "He adopted his niece as a daughter. And if *she* should also suffer some misfortune, he gave his possessions to Glaukon, his homometric brother. And he wrote these things in a will," with, "He adopted Chairestratos as a son. And he wrote thus in a will, if a son was not born to him by his wife, he (Chairestratos) was to inherit his possessions." (6.6-7) More importantly, another client of Isaeus says, "He did not adopt me, writing it in a will when he was about to die, the way others do, nor in sickness, but being in good health and sound mind, he adopted me and introduced me among his phratry." (2.14) Thus we can judge that normal practice during a crisis of health was to adopt by will, and I think that the same thing would be true in a crisis such as Hagnias faced. This is certainly what happened in Isaeus' cases involving Philoktemon, Apollodoros, and Astyphilos.[21] In all three instances the deceased left (or was alleged to have left) a will adopting an heir when he was about to go on a dangerous journey. So, if Hagnias actually adopted the girl, I think that he did so by will. And, if the adoption was a fraud engineered by Glaukos and Glaukon, it was certainly easier to fake a will rather than present witnesses to an adoption that never took place.[22]

---

[20] Perhaps he really wanted to adopt a close friend who was an only son. He could adopt the girl instead and name the friend as her future husband.

[21] 6.5-7, 7.9, and 9.1-6.

[22] Another reason for thinking that the girl was adopted by will is

Secondly, was the will probated? Wyse does not seem able to make up his mind on this point, but only natural descendants or children adopted *inter vivos* could legally enter into possession of an estate without first filing a claim with the archon.[23] Furthermore, we learn from the depositions preserved with Sositheos' speech (43-45) that Euboulides lodged some sort of claim to Hagnias' estate. If this case went to the jury, their verdict against him would ratify the will. (On the nature of this suit see the commentary on the next section.)

Was the will genuine? I think that it was, for Euboulides got nowhere with his claim, and the girl remained in possession of Hagnias' property for the rest of her life. For the eventual overthrow of the will see the next section.

9. Since one of the depositions appended to Sositheos' speech (31) includes the information that Phylomache was awarded the estate of Hagnias during the archonship of Nikophemos, i.e., the year 361/0, the general opinion used to be that Hagnias perished in the war between Athens and Sparta that lasted from 378 to 371, the so-called Theban War. Now, however, the discovery of the *Hellenica Oxyrhynchia* has changed all that. As we have noted, its author dates Hagnias' death to about 396. Unless we are going to reject the evidence of the deposition, we must now reconstruct the chronology of the case somewhat along the following lines. When Hagnias died in (or near) 396, his adopted daughter came into possession of his estate. At that point Euboulides made trouble of some sort for Glaukon (cf. Sos. 43-45). Within the next ten years Euboulides died, then the girl, and Glaukon took over the estate on the basis of Hagnias' will. The gap between 385 and 361 can be partially filled by supposing that Phylomache was an infant when her father died, and the rest perhaps by some negotiating between her husband and Glaukon and by Sositheos' preparations for breaking the will. I find this an acceptable timetable, but many scholars reject the accuracy or authenticity of the deposition.[24]

Theopompos' statement that he *never* challenged the will. Had he said, "Glaukon took the estate in accordance with the will, and we did not challenge the will," that would have meant that the will did not become operative until then, but "never" (οὐδεπώποτ') suggests that neither during the girl's tenure nor Glaukon's did Theopompos raise an objection.

[23] Harrison, I, 156-162. Of course, violations of this rule did occur; cf. Isaeus 9.3 and Ps.-Dem. 48.1-27.

[24] Richard F. Wevers, *Isaeus: Chronology, Prosopography, and Social*

According to Wyse, when Isaeus says, "Euboulides died, and the daughter died," "The audience would inevitably infer from this sentence that Eubulides II died before the adopted daughter of Hagnias II. Sositheus does not give the date of the death of his father-in-law ([Dem.] 43. 55), but three of his witnesses (§§ 43-45) mention the fact that Eubulides claimed the estate of Hagnias as next-of-kin (κατὰ γένος), and that no other person at that time put forward a claim on this ground. Any one who is anxious to white-wash Isaeus may contend either that the depositions in [Dem.] 43 are forgeries, or that Eubulides II unsuccessfully assailed the testament immediately after the decease of Hagnias II, the corruption προσκλαίουσα in [Dem.] 43. 43 concealing the name of the adopted daughter. I prefer the commonplace solution of the difficulty," i.e., once more Isaeus is lying. But what could he gain from reversing the order of these deaths? If his aim is to suppress the fact that Euboulides filed a claim, he has accomplished that simply by not mentioning it. Moreover, in this speech Isaeus tries to hide the claim of Euboulides and his daughter to the estate through the *maternal* line. Thus he could freely admit that Euboulides lodged a claim, by making it appear that he was relying on a *paternal* connection. Consider the paragraph as it stands, but with one alteration; transpose "Euboulides died" and you would have the following: "the girl died, Glaukon took the estate in accordance with the will; we did not think it right to dispute him, but Euboulides did. He then died, and his daughter won the estate; thereupon Stratios, Stratokles, and I prepared to claim, but they died before filing." This certainly would accomplish Isaeus' purpose of showing why Theopompos is the sole remaining rightful heir, yet make no damaging admission about Phylomache. I conclude, therefore, that Isaeus had no reason to lie and that Euboulides did predecease the girl.

As Wyse notes, three of Sositheos' depositions (43-45) say that

---

History (The Hague, 1969), 9-33, argues on stylistic grounds that the speech does belong c. 360. J. K. Davies, *Athenian Propertied Families 600-300 B.C.* (Oxford, 1971), 82-83, eliminates the chronological difficulties by positing that the girl grew up, got married, and had a son. The problem with this suggestion is to imagine how Glaukon could expect to wrest the estate from this boy by producing Hagnias' will. It might help to suppose that the girl grew up but bore no children who survived. That would still leave us to wonder which of Hagnias' relatives claimed her in marriage, unless he named her husband in his will.

Euboulides disputed the estate of Hagnias on grounds of kinship. One of them, in fact, seems to say that he contested the estate with Glaukon, for the corrupt reading of the mss. at § 45, προσκλαίουσα, is most easily changed to πρὸς Γλαύκωνα, "against Glaukon." Either he challenged the validity of the will or else claimed the right to marry the girl (when she matured)[25] and to take the estate, since that was the right of the nearest relative of the deceased. Maybe Glaukon replied that he was entitled to marry the girl. In any event, whether through death, defeat, or compromise, Euboulides did not win his case.

Just what does Theopompos mean by saying that Glaukon took the estate? As Wyse suggests, "If the will of Hagnias II had been approved by the judges immediately after the testator's decease, it is conceivable that on the death of the adopted daughter Glaucon at once entered into occupation of the property without going again before a court, and was then summoned by Eubulides II to disclose and defend his title. This is the conclusion suggested by the words of Theopompus." I would agree here with Wyse, except that it was Phylomache II, not her father, who brought suit, and the defendant might have been Glaukos, since Sositheos (7) calls him "the one previously defeated." But, as usual, Wyse is suspicious and tries to find discrepancies between the versions of Theopompos and Sositheos. "The narrative of Sositheus, though vague, leaves on my mind a different impression, that the estate became vacant (ἔρημος, III. 61), and was claimed by the parties under the ordinary rules; observe [Dem.] 43. 5." There Sositheos says, "At that time Theopompos was at Athens but when the herald announced that if anyone wanted to dispute or place a deposit in connection with the estate of Hagnias either through kinship or a will, he did not dare to make a deposit but gave judgement himself that he had no connection with the estate of Hagnias from any source." There is no other reference in ancient literature to a herald's invitation to contest an estate, but we do learn from Aristotle's *Constitution of the Athenians* that during the main assembly of each month "it is necessary to read out the claims upon the estates and the heiresses so that it will not go unnoticed that one has become vacant." (43.4)

---

[25] Perhaps he was trying to establish himself as her guardian, since her *kyrios* was required to marry her according to the law cited at Ps.-Dem. 46.18. As Harrison notes, I, 138, it is not certain whether an *epikleros* could be claimed in advance of puberty or how her guardian was selected.

Since it does not matter to either speaker's case whether Glaukon actually took possession of the estate, we ought to reconcile the two accounts instead of looking for deception. Perhaps Sositheos has merely simplified his narrative by conflating two trials, the first against *Glaukos* for, say, perjury or forgery in connection with the will, then after the estate was declared vacant and the herald made his announcement, a second, in which Phylomache won control of the estate herself. Theopompos, surprised by the first verdict, did not have time to put in a claim of his own at this time but managed to do so some time later. On the other hand, it seems likely to me that the Athenians would be as anxious to publicize allegations that an estate had been wrongfully awarded as they were to advertize vacant estates. It would serve the interests of the deceased to transform a contest between tenant and challenger into a free-for-all in which anyone could seek the inheritance. So the situation may have been this: Glaukos and Glaukon had been in effective control of Hagnias' property through the girl, the heiress by adoption. When she died, Glaukon entered into possession of the estate without seeking approval of the court. Taking advantage of the law which he cites at section 16, Sositheos then sued to overturn the will, and a herald invited further challengers. Phylomache proved victorious. Either reconstruction would fit both accounts of the proceedings.

We cannot, of course, determine why one jury approved the will while a later one disapproved it, but my own opinion on this follows these lines. It seems clear that, once a will was probated, it was up to the *heir* to retain the will as proof of his inheritance against all comers.[26] That is, neither the court nor the archon kept a copy. Under normal circumstances this would work out perfectly well, for once the heir died, his own heirs would inherit the property. But in the unusual case of a girl adopted by will there was always the possibility that she might die before marrying. In that event the effect of the will was nullified, and the property would revert to the original owner's nearest relative. This would be one reason for naming a contingent legatee. If Glaukos and Glaukon had control of Hagnias' will, they would have had the opportunity

[26] Demosthenes demanded of his guardians that they show him his father's will (27.40-41); he did not go to a Central Records Office. It is in keeping with the self-help nature of Athenian justice that parties had to keep records for themselves.

of forging a new will or adding a codicil to the old one, naming Glaukon as the heir. Perhaps Hagnias actually did name Glaukon as his heir, but the jury must have been suspicious when he produced a document in his own favor. Sositheos could point out the anomaly that Hagnias adopted a daughter when it was possible to adopt a son. This would be an argument that Hagnias did not really like Glaukon and so would not have named him as the contingent heir. I think that in cases involving wills the burden of proof was on the party who benefitted from the will and not on the one who sought to overturn it.[27] So even though Glaukon may have produced a genuine document, he was unable to prove its authenticity and lost his case.

Sositheos tells the jury that when Phylomache sued Glaukon, Theopompos appeared as a witness for Glaukon (§ 4), but before we can make any judgements on Theopompos' conduct we must first know what his testimony there was. Sositheos indicates that it was the most important part of Glaukon's case, but we cannot know this for certain. Indeed Theopompos may have sworn that he saw what Hagnias wrote in his will or heard about it from his very lips. On the other hand, in Athenian court cases witnesses sometimes testified only that they had seen the deceased make a will and that they recognized his seal when the document was later presented for probate. They disclaim, however, knowledge of the contents of the will. Perhaps this was Theopompos' position. Or conceivably he only testified to the good relations existing between the half-brothers. Whatever the case, we have no way of telling whether he was committing perjury or not.

Why did Theopompos support Glaukon? If we are too cynical to admit the possibility that he (rightly or wrongly) believed that Hagnias had in fact named Glaukon as his contingent heir, we can adopt Sositheos' allegation (4) that Theopompos conspired with the brothers. For a motive, we can conjecture that the three agreed to divide the estate equally among themselves. But why should Theopompos settle for a third when he eventually got it all? At the time that Glaukon obtained control of the estate three other

---

[27] The jury probably felt that there were two legitimate heirs, the nearest relative and the testamentary legatee. Therefore, if they could not be sure that the claimant actually was the deceased's choice to succeed him, they would turn to the other (uncontested) legitimate heir. Cf. Isaeus' argument at 1.41-43.

claimants were alive, Stratios, Stratokles, and Phylomache. Even allowing that her claim was invalid, her opponents may have realized that it would be difficult to disprove when she was in position to recruit (or suborn) several favorable witnesses. Therefore, they might have reason to compromise their own conflicting interests in order to eliminate her and the other second cousins. That would be true, whether or not the will was genuine.

Whatever the reason for Theopompos' conduct, we should notice how lightly Isaeus skips over that trial, neither explaining why the will was broken nor implicating his client in that losing venture. Yet he still manages to depict Theopompos as one who supported the deceased's wishes, even to his own disadvantage, and who moved to assert his own rights only after the court had acted, and then only to oust an imposter. (Reverence for the dead so influenced juries that occasionally rival heirs vied for control of the corpse in order to be the one to carry out the funeral rites, while respect for Hagnias is the main pillar of Sositheos' own case.[28])

Why, according to Theopompos, was Phylomache outside the line of succession? She claimed to be a first cousin once removed to Hagnias, but Sositheos (29) says, "Theopompos perpetrated a gigantic lie on the jurors about [the elder] Phylomache, that she was not Polemon's full sister." He may have said that they were not related at all, or that they had the same mother but a different father. This latter charge is made in two cases which have come down to us, Isaeus 12 and Oxyrhynchus Papyrus no. 2538.[29] If Phylomache did not have the same father as Polemon, that would sever the legal connection between her and Polemon's own son Hagnias. It is also possible that Theopompos admitted her paternity but challenged her legitimacy, since under Athenian law bastards could not inherit. Schömann, for one, thinks that the depositions offered by Sositheos prove that Phylomache was the legitimate daughter of Hagnias' grandfather,[30] but Theopompos must have been able to offer witnesses of his own, and surely the jury was better able to determine the truth of the matter than we are. Sositheos says that the attack on her position came as a surprise

[28] Isaeus 8.21-27 and 38-39; cf. also Isaeus 2.36, 4.19, 6.40, and 9.4-5, as well as Ps.-Dem. 44.32 and 48.6-12.

[29] Cf. my article, "An Oratorical Fragment, POxy. 2538," Riv. Fil. 98 (1968), 149-150.

[30] *Op. cit.*, 461; cf. Sos. 35-37 and 42-46.

to him and that as a result he was unprepared in the earlier trial to establish her legitimacy. This is hard to believe, for if she were the legitimate daughter of Hagnias I, her descendants outranked all other claimants. What other strategy did Sositheos expect his opponents to adopt but to question her parentage? He, of course, suppresses the fact that one of his wife's opponents was Hagnias' own mother, who must have seemed to the jury especially qualified to say whether or not Phylomache was her husband's full sister.

Theopompos' position, then, in the previous contest was that Phylomache was outside the line of succession because her grandmother was not the daughter of Polemon or because she was his bastard. In the present trial, however, he leaves an entirely different impression. He is, of course, obliged to mention the younger Phylomache in order to explain how he first came into possession of Hagnias' estate, but in doing so he is δεινός. Any juror without previous knowledge of the case would think that the daughter of Euboulides claimed the estate as the child of a *second* cousin. Her defeat would, therefore, serve as a precedent for rejecting his ward's claim.

It is noteworthy that here and elsewhere Theopompos treats the actual contestants, Phylomache for instance, not as individuals but as members of a faction. (Cf. sections 16-18, 25, 28-30, and 43.)

10. What is the reason for saying that "we were all preparing to file"? Wyse notes that "One of the points which Sositheus makes against Theopompus is that he was the only second cousin of Hagnias II who put in a claim." Sositheos does indeed make an effective thrust, leaving the implication that the rest of the family accepted the position of the elder Phylomache and putting Makartatos on the defensive. (20) All he could do was to make what must have seemed a rather feeble excuse, that the other claimants had died before filing their petitions. But did Sositheos make the same point in his contest with Theopompos? I doubt it, for the claims of Glaukon, Glaukos, and Hagnias' mother would refute the implication that the family recognized Phylomache, and the first jury (unlike the later one) would be well aware that Stratios and Stratokles had recently died. In any event, Theopompos has now disposed of Phylomache and should be concentrating on his nephew's claims. So I judge that his assertion here is designed to score points against *him*, not to answer Phylomache. In general, aside from any possible subterfuge or prevarication, the entire section

(8-10) serves to explain (a) Theopompos' legal claim to Hagnias' estate and (b) why there are no others with equal rights to it. Giving numerous details, such as the preparations for filing, adds verisimilitude to the narrative. And there is an additional point which Theopompos hopes to establish: to counter the claim that he was acting on behalf of his nephew in pressing the case against Phylomache, he says here that Stratios and Stratokles were handling their own claims.

Again, commenting on Theopompos' claim to be the only ἀνεψιοῦ παῖς remaining, Wyse says, "Here we have at last the piece of jugglery with which Isaeus practised on the simplicity of a popular tribunal. Undoubtedly Hagnias II and Theopompus were children of first cousins (§ 8. 3 ἐξ ἀνεψιῶν ἐσμεν γεγονότες), but Theopompus was not the son of the first cousin of Hagnias II (ἀνεψιοῦ παῖς Ἁγνίου πρὸς πατρός), but the son of the first cousin of *the father* of Hagnias II, and consequently had no right to the privileges conceded by the law to ἀνεψιῶν παῖδες. It is astonishing that such a quibble should have won a man a fortune." This last sentence gives the game away, or at least it should. Since it is indeed "astonishing that such a quibble" should succeed, the sensible thing would be to recognize that ἀνεψιῶν παῖδες are second cousins.

Second cousins are, reciprocally, ἀνεψιῶν παῖδες (sons of cousins) to one another, but Wyse here criticizes Theopompos for calling himself ἀνεψιοῦ παῖς (son of a cousin). But what was his alternative? 'Ανεψιῶν παῖς, son of cousins? Actually there is no satisfactory way of expressing this relationship, and a Greek would seldom have need to do so.[31]

11. Isaeus now interrupts his narrative to present a portion of his proof. The literary critic Dionysius of Halicarnassus notes that Isaeus sometimes does this and conjectures that he fears "that his speech will be hard to follow and will overflow on account of the number of its headings and that the proofs, all brought together into one place, being numerous and concerned with numerous matters, may disturb the clarity." (14) So in this speech he keeps separate the proofs on two main issues, presenting here his argument that his nephew has no share in Hagnias' estate, and reserving

---

[31] In discussing the reciprocal, ἀνεψιοὶ ἐκ πατραδέλφων, "cousins from uncles," Wyse (394-395) suggests that a natural way of forming the singular is "cousin from uncle," the type of formation Isaeus employs.

until later (20-31) his involved demonstration that he did not agree to give his ward a portion of the prize.

Wyse says, "Theopompus quietly identifies his rights with those of the ἀνεψιῶν παῖδες designated in the law." He does indeed, and quite rightly since the term means second cousins. Again the commentator: "Why Isaeus here ignores the paternal uncles and aunts of the deceased is manifest." Rather, what is manifest is Wyse's bias against the orator. Hagnias had no paternal uncles and his alleged paternal aunt, Phylomache I, never filed a claim. Here Theopompos is arguing against his ward, not making a veiled allusion to the younger Phylomache.

The law which the clerk read the jury specified that, failing paternal second cousins (or closer relatives), maternal relatives were to inherit. (Sos. 51) Most editors think that the law given in the ms. at this point was reconstructed by an ancient editor or Byzantine scholar on the basis of Isaeus' paraphrase and does not represent what was actually read out in court.

12. Despite the fact that ἀνεψιαδοῦς normally means (and linguistically should mean) son of a cousin, i.e., first cousin once removed, Theopompos here must be using it to mean second cousin, since his point is not that the offspring of first cousins once removed are excluded but that the children of *second cousins*, such as his ward, are excluded from the line of succession. This usage is supported by the grammarian Pollux (3.28) but cannot be demonstrated anywhere else in Attic prose. Again I think that this laxness is attributable in part to Isaeus' desire for variation. He wanted to avoid saying ἀνεψιῶν παῖδες again, but I also think that this term was archaic and seldom, if ever, used in ordinary speech, which would make the lapse that much more natural.

When Theopompos says, "if *we* do not exist" and "*our* children," he means second cousins such as Stratios, Stratokles, and himself.

Jebb construes ἦν ὑπειρημένον as "said *by way of preliminary definition.*" Even though he gives examples of this meaning in other authors, there is nothing preliminary about the first part of the inheritance law in specifying the order of succession in the male line. I take the participle to mean "already said," just as τὸ ὕπαρχον means "that which is *already* in existence," and the tense of ἦν as an example of the Greek idiom in which the imperfect signifies something which has been settled by previous discussion.[32] So in

[32] W. W. Goodwin, *Syntax of the Moods and Tenses of the Greek Verb* (London, 1889), § 40.

English we would say, "as we have seen, the law provides . . . ," but Greek has "as the law provided." Thus in section 4 of this speech we find "the law gave [not gives] the succession" and here, "as was said" rather than "as is said" in the law.

The exact sense of the final sentence is disputed, but clearly we have an *argumentum a fortiori*:[33] if Theopompos, the last of the second cousins, had predeceased Hagnias' adopted daughter, the estate would have gone to Hagnias' maternal relatives.

13-14. Wyse says, "Apparently Isaeus wished to avoid writing καὶ γὰρ ὁ τούτου πατὴρ ταὐτὸν ἐμοὶ προσῆκεν [his father bore the same relationship to Hagnias as I] or καὶ γὰρ ὁ τούτου πατὴρ ἐμὸς ἦν ἀδελφός [his father was my brother]," and typically concludes, "The source of the verbosity is the rottenness of Theopompus' case." Just how reminding the jury that his ward was his nephew would expose the "rottenness" of his case eludes me. The problem here stems from the style of argument preferred in Athenian courts. It is not sufficient to produce eye-witnesses, a speaker must argue from probability to confirm their testimony. Likewise it is not sufficient to quote laws, one must embroider them with rhetorical devices. First, Isaeus establishes the general proposition that, if his nephews (and nieces) are not entitled to a share of the estate even if Theopompos had died, they certainly are not entitled while he is still alive. Then, he uses this conclusion as the major premise of a syllogism, since that form of argument will strike the hearer as ironclad. If the children of second cousins are not eligible to inherit, then the ward is excluded because his father was a second cousin. It is worth noticing that in going from the major to the minor premise of a syllogism, Plato frequently uses the same particles Isaeus uses here, ἀλλὰ μήν.[34] Isaeus uses the same combination later (26) when restating previous conclusions as his premises in a non-syllogistic argument. The effect is, "Well, then, ..."

Theopompos says in effect that there is a right way and a wrong way to settle the ownership of the estate. The proper way was a trial devoted to this single issue, and that in one or the other of two *fora*. First of all, his fellow guardian had the opportunity to join the case against Phylomache but failed to do so. (Theopompos makes this point in 13, 15, 26, and 27.) Even though he forfeited this

---

[33] Cf. Aristotle, *Rhetoric* 1397b, the argument from "the more and the less."

[34] J. D. Denniston, *The Greek Particles* (Oxford, 1959), 346.

chance, his ward is still free to lodge a claim to the estate at any time (a point repeated in sections 14, 19, 26, 27, and 33). Athenian law permitted claims to be filed even after an estate had been awarded. The claimant was required to make a deposit in the amount of one-tenth of the value of the estate, forfeit in the event of defeat.[35] The possessor was obliged to defend his title, or the award was invalidated. That is how Theopompos dispossessed Phylomache, how Sositheos sought to oust Theopompos' son, and how the other guardian should have proceeded in this case, according to Theopompos. Such a suit would not subject the defendant to personal penalty if he lost. Instead, his opponent has brought other matters into the case, such as Theopompos' alleged promise, and changed a civil matter into a criminal case, subjecting him to possible severe sanctions.[36] The motive for this course of action, as set forth in section 31, is to eliminate Theopompos as the boy's guardian so that the opponent, as sole guardian, may embezzle the boy's property.

The fact that the ward did not join in the attack on Phylomache is only partial proof that he recognized the baselessness of his claim, for, as Wyse notes, the guardian could say that he stayed out of that case "because Theopompus promised to give half the property to the ward." In actual fact, of course, the ward could not have hoped to win the estate for himself, regardless of any deal Theopompos was willing to make. He was entirely outside the line of succession.

An Athenian speaker will often tell the jury that they have done something when he means that an earlier jury has done it. Of course, juries were considered representative of the whole Athenian people, and it was politic to remind them from time to time that the majesty of the Athenian *demos* had already bestowed Hagnias' estate on Theopompos.

It is also a frequent device of the orators to start a question with, "Is it not dreadful that," or "Would it not be dreadful if," and then to continue by describing some inconsistent behaviour by their opponents.[37] They regularly employ antithesis between what he

---

35 Cf. Sos. 16 and Pollux 8.39.

36 He turns to this theme in §§ 32-35.

37 See Isaeus 1.38, 1.51, 5.34, 6.58, and 10.23; cf. also 2.42-43 and J. J. Bateman, "Some Aspects of Lysias' Argumentation," Phoenix 16 (1962), 157-177.

should do (μέν) and what he does do (δέ). Here the inconsistency is two-fold: after failing to claim the estate at the proper time he brings up the matter at the wrong time and in the wrong place, and, while he admits that Theopompos has not misappropriated his ward's own funds (his own paternal inheritance), he alleges that Theopompos is stealing his own money, another *a fortiori* argument.

To close this section of the speech Isaeus has written his client a purple passage full of emotive words, such as τολμᾶν, συκοφαντεῖν, and παρασκευάζειν, which implies trumping up false charges and suborning witnesses. By its great length and complexity the period builds from the indignant particle οὔκουν up to a climax in the cry of "shame".

15. Theopompos now resumes the narrative, marking the transition by the combination of particles μὲν οὖν . . . δέ, a regular feature of Greek prose. As Denniston says, "Often the μέν clause sums up and rounds off the old topic, while the δέ clause introduces the new one."[38]

Theopompos again raises the point that his opponent did not present his ward's case at the proper time (he did not enter a deposit worth ten per cent of his claim in order to enter the challenge to Phylomache) and now adds the fact that the sons of Stratios, who have as good (or as bad) a claim as the ward, did not place such a deposit either. Then follows a lacuna in the text which can be filled in one of several ways. In general, the meaning must be either "<for no other reason than the fact that> they recognized their lack of a case" or "nor did they think that they had a case <on the ground of kinship> or any other grounds." I prefer the former since it is a common Greek idiom, but there seems to be no decisive argument either way. In either case I construe the subject of "they think" to be both the opponent and the sons of Stratios. For in the next section Theopompos says, "They, then, as I said, knowing that they were outside the line of succession, did not dispute but kept silence." Since the particles μὲν οὖν show once again that Theopompos is summing up the previous discussion without adding anything new, he is referring to the same people in both sections, and in 16 he seems to be contrasting *all* the parties who acted (δ') with *all* the parties who kept still (μὲν οὖν).[39]

---

[38] *Op. cit.*, 472.

[39] This consideration would rule out the simplest correction yet proposed, οὔτε to οὐδέ (suggested by Baiter and Sauppe in their 1840 edition): "neither

Wyse says that "These sections [15-19] are a remarkable instance of the boldness with which Isaeus will pervert the truth. If the speech of Sositheus had not been preserved, who would have divined from this narrative that Theopompus opposed and defeated Glaucon and Glaucus his late allies?" If this is deemed to weaken Theopompos' claim to the estate once held by Phylomache, what must we say about her husband, who hides the fact that Hagnias' own mother opposed Phylomache's pretensions?

16. Jebb interprets: " 'since even the prosecutor would not be vexing me now ...': *i.e.* as on the *former* occasion the sons of Stratius refrained from litigation, so the son of Stratocles would refrain *now*, did not this pettifogger instigate him ...." But I take the logic (such as it is)[40] to be: my opponent did not intervene before, because he knew that he had no case, since not even a person as wicked as he would intervene now, if I gave him free reign to pilfer (alluding once more to his charge that the other guardian is trying to eliminate him as a guardian in order to gain sole trusteeship and defraud the ward; cf. § 31).

The text, as preserved in the ms., seems to say that Phylomache II "is properly related [to Hagnias] in the same respect as the son of Stratios." That is, although she claims to be something she is not (a first cousin once removed), she is *properly* (δικαίως) a second cousin once removed. Since Stratios had two sons, we can correct the singular to the plural or alter the name to read "the son of Stratokles." It would suit Theopompos' case to make the point that Phylomache, who lost her claim, was in the same position as his present opponent, but nowhere else does he call him the son of Stratokles. Perhaps the solution is that Theopompos said that Phylomache was related to Hagnias in the same way as both his ward *and* the sons of Stratios.

Wyse maintains that the plural οἱ κύριοι cannot stand for the singular, so that Theopompos means her sons and not her husband.

---

did the guardian file, nor the sons of Stratios, who bear the same relationship to Hagnias, *and not* for any other reason did they think that they had a case." The thought is difficult but not impossible: the sons of Stratios did not file, although they had the same relationship as Theopompos' ward, nor did they think that they had a case for any other reason besides kinship. But this would make the sons of Stratios the sole subject of "did they think."

[40] That is, the fact that the opponent would not be suing *now* proves that he knew that he had no case *then*. But why would he not be suing now? Because he knows that he has no case.

That would mean that Glauketes had died and the widow's sons were representing her. Yet we have seen that Isaeus regularly treats the principals in the case not as individuals but as members of a group. For instance, in sections 9 and 18 he speaks of "those disputing according to the will," although Glaukon alone was the testamentary heir. And, strictly speaking, Sositheos was the one "acting on behalf of Euboulides' daughter." (Cf. also the reference to him in the next section.) In reality it appears that a man called Eupolemos represented Hagnias' mother. At any rate, Sositheos says that he, Theopompos, the two brothers, and Eupolemos all spoke at the trial, but the jurors had only four urns in which to cast their votes. (7-10) This should mean that two parties had an identical claim to the estate, apparently Glaukos and Glaukon as half-brothers. This leaves Eupolemos to speak on behalf of the mother, whether as her third husband or because her actual guardians, her sons, had their own case to argue.

Isaeus apparently found it too damaging to mention the brothers' claim. He would be hard pressed to explain why his client opposed them contrary to the intent of the will. Sositheos, however, asserts that the three of them were working together, not in opposition.

17. In filing an answer to Theopompos' suit, Phylomache's husband claimed that she was a first cousin once removed to Hagnias since her paternal grandmother, Phylomache I, was a sister of Polemon, Hagnias' father. Theopompos and (manifestly) Hagnias' own mother proved to the satisfaction of the jury that the elder Phylomache was not Polemon's full sister. Whether they alleged that she was a half-sister or not related at all, we do not know. (See the commentary on 9.) Sositheos (7) charges that Theopompos and Hagnias' half-brothers conspired against Phylomache, but he is careful not to mention that Hagnias' mother must have been part of this frame-up. In any case, Theopompos does not want to bring up old issues that have been settled, so he explains his position as succinctly as possible. That way he does not confuse the question at hand and does not raise doubts about the justness of his previous victory.

In section 8 Theopompos says that he, Hagnias, Euboulides, Stratokles, and Stratios were second cousins, whose fathers were cousins, born of brothers. Stratios' sister, then, was also a second cousin to her own son, Hagnias. According to Theopompos, he outranked her, but Wyse has his doubts. Yet, once again, what good would it do him to lie on this point? If her failure to file as a second cousin casts doubt on the right of a male second cousin to inherit, all he had to do was to suppress the fact that she was her son's second cousin. Athenian law recognized two contradictory principles, those of representation and masculine preference: "males and the sons of males are to prevail, if they are from the same (ancestors), even if they are further removed in kinship." (Cf. Sos. 51 and Isaeus 7.20.) Under the first Theopompos and the woman would take equal shares as representatives of their fathers, but the second must have prevailed in this case. There is some doubt, though, about the meaning of the phrase which I translate, "if they are from the same (ancestors)," ἐκ τῶν αὐτῶν. Here I follow Wyse almost completely when he explains, "Successions at Athens were arranged according to a sequence of stocks. The first place was assigned to the descendants of the deceased, stock A, the second to the descendants of the father of the deceased, stock B, the third to the descendants of the paternal grandfather of the deceased, stock C." (565) I would make only one material change in this statement of the position.[41] Since second cousins are included in the line of succession, the ultimate ancestor is the great-grandfather. So I take it that "from the same (ancestors)" refers to the fountainhead through whom the claimant is connected with the deceased, namely, the deceased himself, his father, his grandfather, or his great-grandfather. In this way a son and his sons outrank a daughter, a brother and his sons outrank a sister, an uncle outranks an aunt, a male first cousin any female first cousin, and a male second cousin any female second cousin. In the paternal line Theopompos and Hagnias' mother are related to Hagnias solely through their great-grandfather Bouselos, so that Theopompos outranks her.

The reason "that Theopompus does not appeal to this law [of masculine priority] against Phylomache II" is, *pace* Wyse, that Theopompos is Hagnias' second cousin, while Phylomache is, in Isaeus' version, only his second cousin once removed. Since they were not related to the deceased in the same degree, there was no need to assert masculine prerogative. The reader is free, therefore, to disregard Wyse's suspicions about Theopompos' failure to do so.

The final sentence of this section reads, "which was the closest of all in nature but is admittedly not in the line of succession."

---

[41] A minor modification: I prefer "inheritance class" to "stock", as indicated in the commentary on section I.

Caillemer suggests a different rendering,[42] that the mother is closest in nature but not the closest within the line of succession, i.e., she ranks, say, fourth or fifth in the line. We must, then, supply the adjective "closest" (συγγενέστατον) in the second half of the sentence. This appears to me almost impossible on philological grounds. Idiomatic Greek for this would be συγγενέστατον τῇ μὲν φύσει, ταῖς δὲ ἀγχιστείαις οὔ. As the particles stand in the text of Isaeus they draw a contrast between the two clauses, "which was nearest in nature" and "is admittedly not in the line of succession." On the other hand, this last phrase or its equivalent, ἔξω τῆς ἀγχιστείας ἐστίν (he is outside the line of succession), is Isaeus' regular way of saying that a person has no right to inherit.[43]

I also interpret section 19 to mean that mothers could not inherit, but in section 29 Isaeus seems to say that they could. We have to take the less natural interpretation someplace. I find it much easier to accept an alternate explanation of 29 than Caillemer's interpretation of this passage. See my comments on §§ 19 and 29.

A problem which has vexed commentators on the present passage is the change from the past tense to the present, "was" to "is". My suggestion is that Theopompos means that the relationship of mother was closest to Hagnias personally when he was alive but is legally excluded from the line of succession.

If everyone agreed that a mother had no right to inherit, why then did Hagnias' mother trouble to file a claim? If her claim was serious, she could only be relying on equity, rather than law, trying to impress the jury that as Hagnias' mother she *deserved* to have his estate. It will not do to say that she filed as both mother and cousin, hoping thereby to gain an advantage. Isaeus' wording is against this view. If that were his point, a simple καί was all that was necessary: "they listed her as mother *also*." Actually I do not think that we can answer this question without answering another. Why did she oppose her sons? To judge from Sositheos' presentation, the case was settled by a plurality of the vote, not a majority. (10) Those who accepted the position of the elder Phylomache would have to vote for her granddaughter, but those who rejected it would split their votes among the mother, the brothers, and Theopompos. The mother then could only siphon votes away from

---

[42] E. Caillemer, *Le Droit de succession légitime à Athènes* (Paris, 1879), 122-123.

[43] Sections 7, 9, 12, 13, 16, 18, 29, and 30.

her sons. Sositheos alleges in section 9 that his opponents conspired to gain four-fifths of the time allotted for speeches. Perhaps they did enter the mother's claim in order to acquire this advantage, but I suggest that the brothers put forward their mother in order to emphasize her opposition to the pretensions of Phylomache. As Polemon's wife, she was certainly in a position to know whether the elder Phylomache was his full sister or not. If she had no legal claim herself, she would not cost her sons votes. In other words, she would be merely a stalking horse. Even though they were basing their case on kinship this time, they were sure to cite the will as one reason for awarding them the estate, hoping that the combination would enable them to defeat the superior claim of Theopompos based on kinship alone.[44] In any event, it was an expensive tactic, for the brothers apparently lost their own deposit and their mother's as well, totalling one-fifth of two talents (cf. § 44, where Theopompos says that the estate is worth that).

18. The text of the ms. apparently means, "Then having described them as second cousins (ἀνεψιοῦ παῖδας), I proved that they too were not in the lines of succession. Thus I established my claim in your court." By changing the first verb, ἐξήλεγξα, to a participle, some editors have eliminated the asyndeton.[45] But that still leaves an important crux, since Theopompos maintains that Phylomache was a second cousin once removed, not a second cousin. One suggested alteration is, "Having described her [Hagnias' mother] as a second cousin (ἀνεψιοῦ παῖδα)," substituting the singular for the plural, but this is pointless, for if Theopompos could defeat her in her capacity as mother, he would not call her something else. Jebb suggests a far more radical change: "Next, when she described herself as the *daughter of a first-cousin* [and no longer *mother* of Hagnias], I proved that *daughters of first-cousins*, too, were not in the succession [since a first-cousin's *son* existed]." Whether his suggestion, ἀνεψιοῦ παιδός, means "daughter of a first cousin" or "second cousin," as I believe, the essential point is that Jebb interprets the phrase "not in the lines of succession" in a relative, not an absolute, sense: with Theopompos alive the woman would be outside the line of succession; with him dead she would be within it. As we have noted, when Theopompos says that someone

---

[44] They probably emphasized the inconsistency between Theopompos' previous support for the will and his present claim.

[45] καί then joins the two participles and no longer means "too".

is outside the line of succession or is not connected (προσήκων) to the deceased, he means that he is more remote than a second cousin and so not entitled to inherit.[46] (He invariably ignores the outside chance that there might be no second cousin or closer kin.) I can find no credible evidence for Jebb's view that a person can be outside the line of succession because someone outranks him.[47] Thus I do not believe that a sister, for example, is outside the *anchisteia* if she has a brother. On the contrary, consider section 30, where Theopompos implies that two people could be within the line of succession, one with a better claim. He says that his ward "could not name a better connection" than Glaukon but was "even outside the line of succession" and adds that Hagnias' mother "*also* was connected to the line of succession." In summary, then, what Theopompos proved was that a mother and a second cousin once removed (Phylomache) were both outside the line of succession, as he normally defines it. Therefore, I follow those editors who print something like, "Having described *myself* as a second cousin, I won the estate." As Wyse says, "Theopompus' restatement of his own title (γράψας ἀνεψιοῦ παῖς εἶναι) helps the judges to understand his case."

From sections 17 and 18 it appears that each of the participants in the prior trial had to specify in writing his relationship to the deceased, but that was unnecessary here (cf. § 6), since the issue now is Theopompos' alleged promise to share Hagnias' estate with his nephew.

19. In this narrative portion of his speech (sections 8-10 and 15-19) Isaeus has provided his client a cogent and concise statement of the history of Hagnias' estate. (Contrast this with Sositheos' long and confusing genealogical exposition, 19-29.) Theopompos shows how he came into possession of it and establishes the legitimacy of that possession by his exposition of the inheritance law, by showing that no other proper claimant remained alive, and by invoking the authority of the judicial system. He brushes aside the fact that Phylomache too once had judicial support for her claim with the explanation that he did not challenge Hagnias' will

---

[46] *Supra*, p. 29, n. 43. For οὐ προσήκων cf. § 3.

[47] Proponents of this interpretation cite Isaeus' speech on the estate of Apollodoros (7.20), where the orator says that "the law gives the right of succession to the males before the females," but this hardly constitutes evidence for what it means to be "inside" or "outside" the *anchisteia*.

out of respect for his wishes. Theopompos makes the issue between Phylomache and himself appear a simple matter of law, and not (as *we* know it was) an acrimonious contention of fact involving the parentage of the elder Phylomache. Thereby he rightly keeps the jury's attention on the present case and gains the added benefit that Phylomache appears to have lost her case as a second cousin once removed. Finally, he shows that the other relatives in this degree did not file a claim to the estate. One can certainly apply to this section the words which Dionysius of Halicarnassus uses to describe Isaeus' style in general (3): pure, accurate, lucid, consisting of ordinary words, vivid, brief, convincing, appropriate to the case, compact, and suited to forensic oratory no less than the style of Lysias.

Normally the narrative section provides a speaker two chances to establish an advantage over his foe.[48] Where they agree on the facts, he can put his own interpretation on those facts, and where there is disagreement about them, sometimes by overwhelming his opponent with numerous questionable accusations and assertions he can get a portion of them accepted by default. As an example of the first, we need consider only how Theopompos and Sositheos treat the fact that Theopompos initially did not file a claim to Hagnias' estate in opposition to Phylomache. For her husband (5) this is a sure sign that Theopompos knew very well the emptiness of his own pretensions, but Isaeus presents the fact as an instance of Theopompos' respect for the wishes of the deceased. As for the second, Lysias' client, the cripple, says that once he has answered the major charges there is no need to address the trivial ones (24.21), but modern propagandists know full well that by using the multiple-lie technique a speaker can get some of his points across.

Although Isaeus uses both tactics to a limited extent, basically his position was not the normal one, for much of his narrative is not directed against an opponent who can rebut him, but goes to justify his claim to the estate, a claim which his ward is in no position to dispute. Actually, then, as between Theopompos and

---

[48] The narrative also gives the writer an opportunity to depict his client's character. As Dionysius of Halicarnassus notes (*Isaeus* 3, 10-12), Isaeus is much weaker than Lysias in this area, and in our case there is little conscious characterization. In fact, it is his strict attention to the matters at hand that sets the tone. As Wyse puts it (676), "Theopompus was able to undertake the rôle of the strong man conscious of his strength, asking for no pity, but nerved to conquer a hostile audience by sheer force of facts and logic."

his present opponent few of the facts are in dispute, nor is their interpretation. Thus there is no need to broadcast numerous lies in order to win acceptance for a few of them. The only major point at issue is whether Theopompos promised half the estate to his nephew. It is here that Isaeus resorts to the usual tactics, giving his own coloration to the fact that neither his opponent nor the sons of Stratios filed a claim, and slipping past the notion that the contest between Theopompos and Phylomache turned on a question of law and not one of fact. In this way he can later use the argument that Theopompos did not have to strike a bargain with his ward to secure testimony against Phylomache. (§ 25)

Even though his task was made easier by the fact that his ward did not dispute his claim to Hagnias' estate, we should not underestimate Isaeus' skill in constructing this narrative. If Theopompos had no right to the estate at all, as most modern scholars think, then the orator has made a silk purse out of a sow's ear. But even granting that Isaeus had merely to present the truth to win his case, we must still admire his work here, for he has presented his material clearly and concisely, leaving no loopholes. In particular, the jury certainly was not filled with the feeling that disturbs modern critics, that Theopompos had cheated Phylomache. And in my view not only has Isaeus done everything that could reasonably be expected of him, he has outdone himself by making Theopompos' case even better than it is, by suggesting that Phylomache lost her claim as a second cousin once removed.

20-21. Reiterating his charges of brazenness, lying, and slandering, Theopompos turns to the second accusation against him related to Hagnias' estate, namely, that he agreed to give half to his ward. As usual, Isaeus employs *a priori* reasoning, showing first that it would be pointless to agree to a division of the property with his brother Stratokles, and then showing the futility of promising a share to his nephew. His initial point is that two litigants who put forth different claims to an estate can strike a bargain so that each will receive a portion, no matter who wins, rather than risk one getting it all and the other none.[49] But two brothers who claim on the same basis will sink or swim together. This is guaranteed by the voting methods employed in inheritance cases, where the members of the jury placed their votes in urns representing different

---

[49] For an actual instance of such an arrangement cf. Ps.-Dem. 48.8.

claims. As Theopompos says, since he and Stratokles had identical legal positions, they would share the same urn. So much for logic. In actual practice Theopompos and Stratokles must have conferred with each other and agreed to act together. Of course, they did not agree to divide the pot if one won and the other lost, but it was open to them to agree to put up a joint front against Phylomache and to recruit witnesses to refute her claim. Part of such an agreement could be, as Theopompos' opponent claims, a provision in favor of his heir should either brother die before final adjudication of the case. Wyse alleges (695) that "A secret arrangement between Theopompus on the one side and his brother's family on the other was a natural precaution, inasmuch as second cousins were excluded from the succession." Once again I can only repeat that what Theopompos and Stratokles had to do was to prove a point of fact (Phylomache's ancestry) and not to fake a point of law.

Wyse raises several other criticisms of Theopompos' version, beginning with his assertion that he and Stratokles were the only ones who were in no position to make a deal. "Glaucon and Glaucus, if they claimed as uterine brothers of Hagnias II, were in exactly the same position as Theopompus and Stratocles." This is merely a quibble, for within the context Theopompos is correct: of the contestants he has mentioned only he and his brother would win or lose together. But there still remains the central question, why does Theopompos not mention the fact that Hagnias' half-brothers were contestants?

Then Wyse remarks, "Phylomache II, who was not a claimant but a tenant defending her possession, would have been very foolish if she made a bargain with the mother of Hagnias II or any other of her assailants." As it turned out, however, Phylomache would have been well advised to strike a deal with Hagnias' mother. As Polemon's wife, her testimony should have carried a lot of weight. If she recognized Phylomache I as Polemon's full sister, that would have been the best possible endorsement of the second Phylomache's claim. Of course, she did not do so.

22. Despite the complexity of this long sentence, it can be understood without tampering by modern editors. (See Wyse's discussion.) Once Stratokles died, the entire estate passed to Theopompos; all he had to do was vindicate his claim against Phylomache. Heretofore there had been no talk of an agreement between the brothers. Only now did the opponent bring it up.

(Theopompos here uses the historical present; apparently he is becoming more animated as he contemplates his opponent's effrontery.) The intent was to fool a jury. (Inventing this "agreement" prepared the way for a challenge to Theopompos.) However, the law allows no room for such maneuvering as the opponent alleges. (It requires each claimant to file separately.) I take it that the other guardian did not merely discuss the alleged compact with Theopompos but began to broadcast it publicly. If the supposed agreement had not been made public until late in the proceedings, Isaeus would have used that as an argument against its genuineness, nor could his opponent reply that it had to be kept secret since it was corrupt or in bad taste.

23. From the jury's point of view Theopompos has done little here except reiterate his charges of brazenness and perjury and repeat himself to the effect that a combination with Stratokles was out of the question. But for us there is one point of interest. Even though we know no more of this law than Theopompos tells us, we can see that claimants had to file their own individual suits even though proceeding on a common basis. This ought to mean that, if they won their suit, the property would be divided equally and would not be held in joint tenancy.

24-25. Having shown that his nephew has no claim to Hagnias' estate, Theopompos now takes up his opponent's allegation that he promised to give half the estate to his nephew anyway. Isaeus' technique here is remarkable. He presents the two halves of the case against his client as the horns of a dilemma, and uses one of his favorite rhetorical devices, *hypophora*, propounding possible alternatives, only to reject each.[50] In effect, Theopompos conducts a dialogue with himself, thereby bringing into a rather slow paced portion of the speech the rapidity of conversational exchange. Other Greek orators sometimes lose this speed by introducing as many as five alternatives,[51] but Isaeus does not make that mistake here.

On the level of formal logic the defect of this procedure is that one cannot be certain that he has listed all the possible alternatives or reasons for an action.[52] But in this instance it is at the practical level that Isaeus misleads the jury. Actually Theopompos did have

---

[50] See 2.21 and 5.45-46; cf. also 3.72, 4.20, and 7.33.

[51] Cf. Andocides 3.14-15.

[52] Cf. John Stuart Mill, *A System of Logic* 3.8.5. For some other examples of this style of argument cf. Isaeus 2.27 and 5.43 and Demosthenes 27.19-22.

need of witnesses to disprove Phylomache's assertion that her grandmother was a full sister of Hagnias' father. Why the subterfuge? Partly, I think, not to ruin the rhetorical effect of this figure. But also it is Isaeus' policy not to drag up the old issue of the elder Phylomache's parentage and to maintain the illusion that Phylomache II lost her case as a second cousin once removed.[53]

An effective weapon in the proof section of this speech is the use of the form of conditional sentence which Gildersleeve has named the logical,[54] for it denotes that the hypothesis inexorably implies the conclusion. Sometimes this is by definition, sometimes tautology. The speaker neither affirms nor denies the hypothesis; he merely says that, *if* it is true, the conclusion *must* follow. Pritchett has observed that this type of conditional sentence is favored by the forensic speakers including Isaeus because of its basic fairness.[55] The contrary-to-fact condition is also popular in argument, but it lacks the logical inevitability of the other, as well as its appearance of impartiality. Consider the beginning of 25, where a Byzantine scribe or critic, by adding the particle ἄν, has wrongly altered the sentence to mean, "if they had no part of the succession, why would I have agreed to give them a share?" It should be, "if they had no part, why *did* I agree?" The first form of expression implies quite clearly that Theopompos did not give them a share and refuses even to entertain the possibility, but the second seems blander and more objective: he at least appears willing to consider the *hypothetical* possibility of an agreement. Again, it is contrary to Isaeus' position to suppose with Wyse that the final sentence of § 25 might mean, "if they had been unwilling to give the testimony which they actually gave, would I have lost?"[56] Rather, the effect is, "Suppose for the sake of argument that they refused to testify, did it follow

---

[53] It was scarcely worthwhile for his opponent to point out that Theopompos *could have* benefitted from testimony by members of the ward's faction, if, in fact, it was never given.

[54] B. L. Gildersleeve, "Studies in Pindaric Syntax," A. J. P. 3 (1882), 435.

[55] W. K. Pritchett, "The Conditional Sentence in Attic Greek," A. J. P. 76 (1955), 6. As Goodwin notes, *op. cit.*, § 404, "This form of condition may be used even when the supposition is notoriously contrary to fact, if the speaker does not wish to imply this by the construction."

[56] This, at least, seems to be the meaning of his comment, "If connexions of Stratocles cooperated in the attack on Phylomache II, the appearance of the imperfect indicative is intelligible."

that I was going to lose?"[57] In this sentence Isaeus is not concerned whether or not they did in fact testify. He is simply considering the logical result of a hypothetical refusal to give testimony.

The effect, then, which Isaeus strives for in this section is to show Theopompos as a severely logical man, dispassionately considering *on its merits* each reason for striking a bargain with his nephew and rejecting each one in turn.

26. The ms. here gives two separate sentences: "if it was not possible ... award (ἀπόδοτε) me the estate," and "if they did not file a claim ... how must one believe their story?" However, modern editors have recognized that section 26 is constructed along the lines of section 19, a series of conditional clauses leading up to a final question. Therefore, they change the imperative ἀπόδοτε to ἀπέδοτε and add a connecting particle (δ').

There is another problem in the text, where the ms. has, "they did not enter a claim upon the same property (τῶν αὐτῶν)." Münscher changes τῶν to τότε:[58] "they did not file a claim *then* nor did they ever think it right to dispute it." This produces the same contrast we find in the next section, i.e., the ward did not join the challenge to Phylomache (*then*) nor did he file a suit against Theopompos *at any time* subsequently.

For his summation Isaeus has chosen to present his main contentions in the form of a long multi-faceted rhetorical question, based once again on the logical conditional form. He summarizes here not only the second part of his defense, that it was not possible to make a deal with Stratokles himself and pointless to make one with his son, but also harkens back to his earlier demonstration that he and he alone is entitled to the inheritance, by reminding the jury that his opponent did not join the suit against Phylomache and has not troubled to file against Theopompos for a share of the estate, and by invoking once more the authority of the previous verdict in Theopompos' favor. The one new point here, which has

---

[57] Wyse is wrong to expect a future condition here. As Goodwin says, *op. cit.*, §§ 407-408, "Even the future indicative with εἰ may be used in a present condition, if it expresses merely a *present* intention or necessity that something should be done hereafter .... It is important to notice that a future indicative of this kind could not be changed to a subjunctive with ἐάν without an entire change of sense and time."

[58] "Isaios," translated by Karl Münscher, Z. f. v. Rechtswissenschaft 37 (1920) [Zugleich *Festgabe für Josef Kohler zum siebzigsten Geburtstage*], 302, n. 1.

gone unemphasized up to this time, is the fact that Stratokles did not and could not pass on any part of Hagnias' estate to his son. No one, apparently, has suggested that he did, and I think that Isaeus raises this point merely to exhaust all the logical possibilities.

27. This next section of the speech might be termed the re-rebuttal,[59] for here Isaeus seeks to rebut the answer which his opponent has made to the orator's own assertions about the failure to join in the attack on Phylomache or file a claim to the estate at any subsequent time. Section 27 shows that Theopompos' opponent made a plea to the jury something like the following: "I have learned [or I suppose] that Theopompos will say that I acknowledged that my ward has no right to Hagnias' estate by my failure to join the challenge to Phylomache or to lodge a claim later. I admit that I did neither of these things, but for a very good reason. Stratokles and Theopompos knew that Phylomache had no right to Hagnias' estate and they agreed to bring suit against her. But Stratokles was in ill health and afraid that he might die before the case was settled. Therefore, relying on the bonds of kinship, the strongest bonds of all, he agreed with Theopompos that, if one of them died, the survivor would work on behalf of the deceased's son and heir. I reminded Theopompos of this agreement after Stratokles did die. Relying on that agreement, I did not file a claim to the estate against Phylomache. When I found that I had been tricked by Theopompos, it was too late to do anything about it. Our ward could not file suit against Theopompos for the estate, since a ward cannot sue his guardian. Therefore, I had to institute proceedings in my own name, not of course for the estate—which does not belong to me—but a suit to punish Theopompos for his bad behaviour toward our ward."

The pronouns in this section are troublesome. When Theopompos mentions the charge that he is the "cause of not filing against them," *them* (ἐκείνους) should certainly refer to Phylomache, since all the claimants had to file against the holder of the estate.[60] Next he says, παρακαταβάλλειν αὐτοῖς, which Wyse apparently takes to mean, "make a deposit along with them." Since *them* could not be Phylomache, who did not have to make a deposit to retain the estate which she already possessed, the word would have to mean "the other clai-

---

[59] The technical term for this section of a speech is ἡ λύσις or αἱ λύσεις.

[60] ἐκείνους should have the same meaning as ἐκείνοις in the next section, but unfortunately § 28 is corrupt, so that we cannot build on it.

mants." But it would be incomprehensible to say, "I am the cause of not filing against them so that on this account they did not make a deposit along with them," if *them* has two different meanings. Therefore, Wyse and some other editors alter αὐτοῖς to αὐτούς, making it the subject of the verb "to make a deposit." The meaning would be, "so that they [the ward and his guardian] did not make a deposit." I think that a better solution is to interpret αὐτοῖς as αὑτοῖς, the reflexive, and to base a translation on Isaeus 4.10, "Realizing that he would be refuted concerning the connection by birth, he abandoned his son's claim and made a deposit on his own behalf on the basis of a will," where the Greek is ἑαυτῷ παρακατ-έβαλεν. The gist of his opponent's argument is that Theopompos sued Phylomache on behalf of the ward as well as himself. Therefore, the ward did not file *on his own behalf*. So I translate, "I am the cause of not filing against them on the grounds that I promised to give a share, so that on this account they did not make a deposit on their own behalf."

According to Wyse, "the language is misleading; truth demands πρὸς ἐμὲ rather than πρὸς ἐκείνους. What the guardian said was 'I did not contest the *claim of Theopompus*, because he gave me a promise that the ward would not suffer'." Actually what Theopompos has in mind is that the ward, being outside the line of succession, was unable to join in challenging Phylomache, as his father had agreed to do.

28-30. The first half of Theopompos' re-rebuttal consists of his statement that no law forbids his ward from asserting his rights to Hagnias' property. Clearly a criminal suit (γραφή or εἰσαγγελία) like this one was in order, but scholars disagree whether Theopompos' opponent could obtain redress for the ward by filing a civil suit (δίκη). Wyse, as usual, thinks that Isaeus is lying, but others support the orator's position. There is no hard evidence to settle the matter, and commentators argue *a priori*. Wyse says, "The question is not settled by Theopompus' challenge to the prosecutor to quote a law forbidding private suits between a ward and a guardian (§ 34). The disability may have existed in the absence of a specific prohibition, being a consequence of the joint-liability of the guardians and the legal incapacity of a minor." (699) I think that the right of one guardian to act independently of another was a grey area, for clearly neither speaker was able to quote a law proving his contention.

The second half of Theopompos' rejoinder is somewhat obscured by textual corruption. The text of the ms. cannot be translated, for ἐλάγχανον should be followed by the genitive, not the accusative, and mean, "lodge a claim to the estate" (interpreting the phrase as ἐλάγχανον δίκην τοῦ κλήρου). Most editors make the required change to the genitive, κλήρου, and obtain something like, "they did not file a claim to the estate against those who were connected with it."[61] But Theopompos must never admit that Phylomache had any legitimate connection with the estate, for she was only a second cousin once removed, in exactly the same position as his present opponent. Rather than correcting the case of τὸν κλῆρον, I prefer the course favored by Wyse and others, who alter the participle προσήκουσι to ἔχουσι, "They did not file a claim against those people, the ones who possessed the estate." Perhaps, though, we should strike out the phrase altogether, as a gloss. A reader may have found the sentence, "They did not file a claim against them," and wondered who *them* was. He would then supply, "the possessors" or "the ones connected with the estate."

Either way, he begins his rebuttal by repeating his initial charge that his opponent failed to file earlier because he had no claim. Wyse, however, citing sections 13 and 15, maintains, "The line of argument hitherto has been that the ward had no right to half the estate, because (among other reasons) his guardian did not oppose Theopompus' claim to the whole. Now, to meet the retort of the guardian that Theopompus induced him to abstain by promising to surrender half the estate to the ward, Isaeus shifts his ground and declares that the guardian did not compete, because his ward had no rights." (698) Actually the thrust of section 13 is the inconsistency in filing suit now after the previous failure to do so, while in 15 Theopompos apparently says the very same thing he says now, in almost identical words. Compare οὐδὲν αὐτοῖς ἐνόμιζον προσήκειν τούτων τῶν χρημάτων with ὅτι οὐδ' ὁτιοῦν αὐτοῖς τούτων τῶν χρημάτων προσῆκεν.[62] The reasoning is never fully stated but seems to be based on the Destructive Hypothetical Syllogism, a favorite method in Athenian speeches.[63] If he had a

[61] This version could also mean, "they did not file against those who were connected with the estate."

[62] We have noted the slight corruption in 15 when discussing that section; whatever the correct emendation, the similarity to 28 is apparent.

[63] Cf. Stanley Wilcox, *The Destructive Hypothetical Syllogism in Greek Logic and in Attic Oratory* (New Haven, 1938).

valid claim, he would have filed; his failure to file implies that he had no valid claim. Implication easily becomes cause: he failed to file *because* he had no valid claim.

But it is not sufficient merely to repeat himself, since his opponent has challenged the proposition that anyone with a valid claim would necessarily have filed. So he has recourse to the *reductio ad absurdum*, granting his opponent's allegation, for the sake of argument, and showing where it would lead. If the ward had brought suit against Theopompos for half of Hagnias' estate and if Theopompos, in effect, had let the case go by default, it would still have been possible for relatives nearer to Hagnias to invoke the procedure which Theopompos and later Sositheos used: "If someone disputes the estate after it has been adjudicated, or the heiress, let him summon the victor to the archon . . . and if, having been summoned, he does not contest, the award of the estate shall be invalid." (Sos. 16) Wyse correctly notes that Theopompos could have *given* half the estate to his ward, rather than letting him win it in court. But Isaeus, of course, suppresses this possibility, for it would have ruined the figure.

Even though we have seen that the natural interpretation of sections 17 and 19 is that a mother was not entitled to inherit, some scholars think that §§ 29-30 show just the opposite. Either, that is, Isaeus is blatantly inconsistent, or we have misconstrued what he said earlier. I prefer to believe that he now means that Hagnias' mother could claim as a second cousin. In that capacity she would outrank Glaukon, but some say that we must take Isaeus literally when he says that *if* Glaukon was unwilling to claim the estate, then his mother could proceed. Apparently, he outranks her. Yet the orator is not writing a law treatise in the manner of Lipsius or Harrison, listing every possible heir in the exact order. Still, if we want to hold Isaeus to his word here, we should bear in mind that he may have been thinking in practical terms. If Glaukon actually controlled his mother, her legal priority would mean nothing. Only if he had a better position, say, as his father's heir, would he permit her to file. In this way it may be possible to interpret what Isaeus says in the strictest sense.

Again, some urge that the final words of 29 show that in the next section Isaeus is concerned with maternal relatives only. While this is the natural interpretation, I do think, on the other hand, that his explanation, "for she too was connected with the line of succession of her son," is otiose if everyone recognized a mother's right to inherit, but quite to the point if he is reminding the jury that she was related to the deceased in a second capacity. I conclude, therefore, that Isaeus is emphasizing the first half of the last sentence of 29, not the second, and is simply stressing that the law excluded second cousins once removed. (The only way to avoid this conclusion is to say that in § 17 Isaeus actually claims that a mother can inherit and that in § 19, when he says that she was not connected to Hagnias in the line of succession, he actually means that she *was* connected but more remotely than Theopompos.) In any event, notice Isaeus' economy here. He could have made things easier for students of Greek law by ignoring the mother and citing, for instance, some maternal cousins as potential claimants. That is what Sositheos might have done, but Isaeus is too accomplished a writer to confuse the jury with additional *dramatis personae.*

31. As in §§ 13-14 Theopompos charges his tormentor with slander, malicious prosecution, and getting up false suits. He also repeats his version of the prosecutor's motives. Just as in section 16, he argues that by eliminating his fellow guardian the villain will be able to defraud the ward. There is one new point here, the prosecutor's immunity from loss. In most Athenian cases, private or public (δίκαι/γραφαί), the prosecutor stood to lose (money or civil rights) if he failed to obtain a certain portion of the votes (usually 20%). This helped to prevent frivilous or malicious suits, but in some areas the Athenians sought to make litigation easier. Thus in cases involving the mistreatment of orphans or heiresses, wrongdoing by public arbitrators, and subversive activities, a man could lay an information (*eisangelia*) before the proper authorities without risk. The other guardian has, therefore, chosen to proceed by this course of action instead of filing a deposit and directly claiming the estate for his ward.[64] That was a good way to lose his deposit. Eventually the process of *eisangelia* became so abused as a costless way of harassment that the Athenians instituted a penalty for failure to secure a fifth of the votes.

32-34. The rhetorical handbooks available to aspiring speakers apparently recommended raising the argument that the trial was being conducted in the wrong forum.[65] This call for a change of

---

[64] Although Theopompos sometimes calls the proceeding a *graphe*, it is nevertheless an *eisangelia*; on this form cf. Harrison, II, 50-59.

[65] Cf. J. C. T. Ernesti, *Lexicon Technologiae Graecorum Rhetoricae* (Leipzig, 1795), s.v. μετάληψις.

venue is termed *metalepsis*. The point of it here is not to quibble about jurisdiction but to raise doubts about the prosecutor's good faith and to secure sympathy for Theopompos on the ground that he is being subjected to a risk inappropriate to the alleged wrong-doing. Isaeus' procedure here is similar to his approach in sections 24-25, where he lists a number of alternative possibilities. In fact, of course, the more options he presents, the fairer he seems. For in that way he does more than complain about his opponent's choice of proceeding, he actually shows what other recourse he had. And for the third time in the speech (cf. §§ 24-25 and § 26) Isaeus uses a series of logical conditions, again for apparent fairness, in which he neither asserts nor denies the premise but simply states the conclusion that must follow from it. The first three alternatives are ones which he has already discussed and, as in section 26, he adds one other possibility just for the sake of completeness.

The jury has been told that it is still possible for anyone with a better claim to challenge Theopompos' possession, just as he challenged Phylomache. The procedure involves going to the archon's court, for he was the protector of defunct family lines, and trying the case before a full jury. Sositheos has the relevant law read out at section 16 of his speech: "If someone disputes the estate after it has been adjudicated, or the heiress, let him summon the victor to the archon, just as in the other private suits. And the disputant is to make deposits. And if, having been summoned, he does not contest, the award of the estate shall be invalid." In this type of case, a *diadikasia*, there was no plaintiff or defendant, but two people asserting a better right, and the jury was to choose between them. Alternatively, the guardian might bring a regular private suit to enforce Theopompos' alleged promise, once again in the archon's court with a full jury. Only this time, the parties would be plaintiff and defendant. (The distinction is repeated in § 34, where ἐπιδικάσασθαι and πρὸς ἐμέ refer to the first form and κατ' ἐμοῦ and δικάσασθαι to the second.)[66] Presumably, the action would be for breach of contract (ὁμολογία), a δίκη βλάβης "suit for injury."[67]

[66] Harrison, II, 79-80.

[67] At any rate, the title of Ps.-Dem. 48, which seeks to enforce a similar agreement, is given in the mss. and by Dionysius of Halicarnassus (*Demosthenes* 13) as κατὰ Ὀλυμπιοδώρου βλάβης. Fritz Pringsheim, *The Greek Law of Sale* (Weimar, 1950), 53, rejects this title, but his argument seems little more than special pleading.

Wyse says, "A contract made for a *causa turpis* was probably void .... The prosecutor would have been ill-advised if he had proceeded against Theopompus under the law of contract." By that he means that neither Theopompos nor Stratokles had a right to the estate. But if they did, as I maintain, perhaps the plaintiff could justify the agreement on the ground that the two fathers wanted to provide protection for their children, if one should die before the estate was adjudicated.

We have already noticed that the prosecutor could not cite a law preventing a ward from bringing a private suit against his guardian, and that Theopompos for his part could cite no authority specifically providing for such an action. Cf. §§ 28-30.

The one new point Isaeus makes in these sections concerns the procedure for managing a ward's property. While it was possible for a guardian to manage it himself, farming the land, lending or investing the money, renting out the slaves, he could also petition the archon to lease the estate to an entrepreneur who would provide a fixed income to the ward and himself risk a loss in the hope of a profit. In another of his speeches Isaeus describes a process whereby the guardians themselves sought the lease for their own account. "They registered these two boys with the archon as adopted ... adding themselves as guardians, and they bid the archon to lease the estates on the ground that they were orphans, in order that in their names some of the estate might be leased, and some become security (and boundary markers be placed) while Euktemon was still alive, and they themselves becoming lessees might receive the income. And when first the court was filled, the archon announced it, and they secured a lease. But some people, being present, reported the plot to their relatives, and coming they revealed the matter to the jurors, and the jurors voted not to lease the estates." (6.36-37) In our case, although Wyse notes the formal possibility that ἀπογραψάσθω πρὸς τὸν ἄρχοντα may mean that the other guardian should register himself as a bidder for the lease, the argument demands, "he should register the ward's portion of Hagnias' estate." If he thinks that the half belongs to the boy, let him register *it* for leasing. In practice, Isaeus' suggestion would be ludicrous; no one would rent property knowing full well that he would have to sue to gain control of it. Nor would the opponent be willing to lay himself open to prosecution by the lessee if the latter could not get satisfaction from Theopompos. But it does make a good debating point.

35. If Theopompos were convicted, the prosecutor would propose a penalty to be inflicted on him, and Theopompos would counter with a milder alternative. The jury would then choose one or the other, just as at the trial of Socrates. We do not know what limit there was in the case at hand, but by σῶμα Theopompos may mean, not that his life was in danger, but that he might suffer some loss of civic rights, such as the right to address the assembly or bring suit.[68]

As in § 14, Theopompos again contrasts his ward's property with his own, but he cannot simply say, "prosecute me if I have his property, leave me alone if I have mine." Simply to be in possession of the ward's property was not criminal; unless he leased it out, a guardian would have to be in possession. Only if he neglected the management of the estate or appropriated the profits for himself, would he be liable. Therefore, Theopompos had to add that proviso to his antithesis.

32-36. Wyse says that Isaeus' opponent has chosen the proper method for redressing his ward's grievances. Certainly the archon chose to accept the course he followed. But there is much to be said for Isaeus' interpretation that the ownership of the estate should be settled on its own merits and not made part of a process where a natural prejudice would work for the ward and against the guardian. And, to the extent that the case concerned the valid interpretation of the inheritance law, to make Theopompos liable to criminal penalties was grotesque. Only if he prevented his ward from suing to vindicate his rights, would he be failing in his duties as guardian.

This unit plays an important part in the overall design of the speech. Theopompos opened his case confidently, expounding the inheritance law. Then in his narrative he had the opportunity to present the facts according to his own lights. But beginning with section 20 he lost the offensive and was forced to answer specific allegations made by his opponent. Now he has reversed their positions: he goes onto the attack, in effect making his opponent the defendant on a charge of bringing an improper suit. This short respite is badly needed, for henceforth Theopompos will usually be on the defensive.[69]

37-38. We come now to the second half of the speech, in which

[68] Cf. Harrison, II, 169-176.

[69] Perhaps, however, at the end of the speech he was able to regain the offensive by showing how he increased his ward's wealth.

Theopompos replies to charges that despite his great wealth he has allowed his wards to languish in need. At the very beginning of the *Rhetoric* (1356a) Aristotle lists three types of persuasion, based, respectively, on character, emotions, and logical argument. Once he had finished his own discussion of the inheritance law and Theopompos' alleged promise, the opponent turned to an extraneous issue in order to exploit the first two of Aristotle's modes, blackening Theopompos' character and arousing the jury's anger against him and pity for Stratokles' children. For a good idea of just how a skilful orator could achieve an effect by contrasting a wealthy family with their poor, orphaned kin, see what Lysias has done in his prosecution of Diogeiton. (32, *passim*) And certainly the jury will begrudge it that *in addition* to his patrimony Theopompos has also acquired Hagnias' estate plus control over the property of his brothers-in-law, Chaireleos and Makartatos, by making his own son Makartatos' heir through posthumous adoption.[70]

Just how Isaeus proposed to counter these tactics we cannot tell, for his speech breaks off before he has gotten very far. Perhaps Theopompos will expand on his own charges that the other guardian was the true despoiler, but his primary tack is more subtle. To combat the appeal to passion he himself becomes dispassionate. He begins by resorting to the device recognized by the rhetoricians as συγχώρησις. Here, as in section 35, he adopts an attitude of sweet reason, accepting there the need to steward his ward's property with fidelity and here the obligation to care for his nieces. He gets right with the jury through embracing their moral attitudes. Then, because he cannot deny his control of three estates, he seeks to minimize their importance and in doing so, I suggest, keeps the jury's attention on minutiae and away from appeals to emotion.

39. Once more we have a long summation of various propositions put in the form of a logical condition. Significantly, in §§ 19 and 26 Theopompos summarizes what he has already established, but in 39 he is setting out the agenda of points to be proven in the rest of the speech. I think that the difference results from the difficulty of comprehending the proof to be offered. Section 19 summarizes a straight-forward narrative, 26 recapitulates narrative and legal exposition; but to refute the accusation that he has neglected his brother's children, it will be necessary to go through a listing of

[70] Theopompos' son will face the same sort of strategy in his contest with Sositheos.

numerous properties and calculations of their value and earning power.[71] Thus Theopompos tells the jury what to listen for, that his ward possessed a larger estate which did not have to be defended against other claimants and that as guardian he himself increased its worth. Unfortunately, the speech breaks off before we reach his treatment of the latter point.

40-43. Isaeus' task is to show how, starting with a patrimony of equal value, Stratokles could outstrip his brother, even though Theopompos acquired two additional estates. To appreciate his problem we have to consider the evidence available to him. Theopompos could supply the value of their inheritance, but there was probably no one left alive to confirm his story. Then, as guardian, Theopompos knew what Stratokles left at his death and the extent of Theophon's estate. He would also have access to any property leases. But unless he could obtain detailed records of Stratokles' affairs extending over a decade or more, he could not know himself just how Stratokles made his money and certainly could not hope to convince a jury about it. He could, therefore, know where his brother started and where he finished but not how he got there.

Isaeus' other problem is that Theopompos is charged with converting his own property to cash, an accusation which by its very nature cannot be refuted. Therefore, even though he might convince the jury that his valuation of the various properties and flocks is accurate, he still cannot *prove* that Stratokles had the larger estate.

Thus he must turn from the actual to the potential and give the jury a *reason* why Stratokles surpassed his brother. It might, in fact, be the case that Stratokles was a superior farmer or businessman, but the jury is scarcely likely to accept that explanation without some evidence to substantiate it. Thus Isaeus raises the argument that it was through control of his brother-in-law's property that Stratokles got ahead of Theopompos. Since there was no way of determining exactly how much Stratokles actually realized from Theophon's estate, the orator has to rely on the principle of *ignotum pro magnifico* and skip lightly over the true way in which Stratokles accumulated his wealth. This procedure is certainly not convincing

[71] Just as he has made it easy for the jury to understand the genealogy involved in the case by omitting inessential persons, so he makes the financial aspects clearer by painstakingly adding or subtracting the various sums he needs to mention. The young Demosthenes uses a similar tactic throughout his first speech; cf. especially 27.9-11 and 35-37.

to the modern reader, but the jury may have been more attuned to the ways a guardian could, legitimately or fraudulently, make a profit from his office. Obviously, since Theopompos and his opponent tax each other with this sin, there must have been the opportunity to cheat one's ward. But it is also possible that Stratokles benefitted in an honest manner. Theopompos describes the estate as worth two and one-half talents while Stratokles controlled it and worth as much after he died. If we accept this, it follows that Theophon allowed him the use of the estate until the girl should marry.[72] Since Theopompos' ward is said to draw a return of more than eight per cent on his real estate, and Demosthenes (27.58) says that a certain ward's estate doubled in six years, it would not be unreasonable to calculate that Stratokles *could* have made a profit of ten per cent each year on the value of Theophon's estate of two and one-half talents. In nine years, at that rate compounded, he would realize about 140%, or three and one-half talents.[73]

---

[72] Demosthenes' father allowed one of the boy's guardians the income from seventy mina as long as he was a minor. (27.5) Perhaps Stratokles received a *quid pro quo* for permitting the adoption. It would be pointless for Isaeus to ascribe money to Stratokles which actually belonged to his daughter. If the money did belong to her, he could harp on that to show how silly it was to help with her dowry. He could then shift from considering the money separately to lumping it all together and achieve much the same rhetorical effect.

[73] If Theopompos is telling anything like the truth, it appears that he and his brother started out with estates of about one talent each. With an income of ten per cent they would have just enough to support their families in comfortable style with little left over. (See A. H. M. Jones, *Athenian Democracy* [Oxford, 1957], 135; Ps.-Dem. 42.22.) When Stratokles took over the farm at Eleusis, he could reinvest all his profits therefrom while continuing to support his family from his own property. At first he drew, say, just ten per cent from his new farm, but he loaned out the profits at a much higher rate of return. Rating the farm and animals at two and one-half talents, we find that the return was two and one-quarter talents in nine years. The profits, if loaned at eighteen per cent (not compounded), would yield one and two-thirds talents by the end of this period. (.18 x .25T x 36 [the sum of the years 1-8] = 1.62T.) It seems likely that Stratokles' nine year tenure ended with his death, but if it ended with his daughter's marriage, he would have even longer to compound his wealth. Toward the end of his life Stratokles sold his ancestral property and used the proceeds and part of his loan capital to purchase a new farm at Thria. That is, once he had accumulated a large fortune, he was able to switch from riskier loans to safer, more prestigious land. This, then, is one way that Stratokles could have made some four talents while Theopompos continued to live off his inheritance of one talent without improving his position. By the time of this trial he had not had Hagnias' property long enough to benefit from it very much.

But then Isaeus is not interested in proof, he is interested in persuasion, and, as far as persuading the jury is concerned, he has provided a far more effective weapon than the mere suggestion that Stratokles could have benefitted greatly from the control of his daughter's legacy. What the orator does is to make Stratokles' estate appear much larger than Theopompos' by describing the one concisely and the other at great length and in great detail, making each discrete item seem equally important, whether it be the large farm at Thria or a few sheep, four thousand drachmai or four hundred.[74]

40. In the Athenian liturgical system the wealthiest citizens were required to perform or finance various public services on an individual basis. A man might train or hire someone to train the chorus for a play at one of the dramatic festivals, he might give a banquet at a religious ceremony, or he might serve as captain and paymaster of a warship. Apparently these obligations were distributed on a relative, rather than an absolute, basis: there was no fixed sum necessary to qualify for these liturgies, and anyone could avoid them by showing that another was wealthier than he.[75] Thus Theopompos' characterization of his inheritance is extremely vague and, therefore, suspicious. Wyse, for one, comments, "Theopompus is reluctant to give a brief inventory of the estate of his father Charidemus. If he had adopted this simple and straight-

[74] The figure is called συναθροισμός, a type of *amplificatio*; cf. Rutilius Lupus 1.2 and Quintilian 8.4.27. Notice also that in §§ 41 and 43 he tries to make the properties seem even more numerous by describing them *asyndeton*. Aristotle observes (*Rhetoric* 1413b) that the conjunction makes many items seem like one, and omitting the conjunction makes one seem like many. Contrast this with Demosthenes' use of καί in 27.9-11.

[75] Many scholars think that there was a fixed minimum, but Harrison, for example, can cite (II, 234-235) only Demosthenes 20.19: "The wealthiest are already always exempt from the *choregia* when they serve as trierarchs, and those who possess less than a suitable amount, having their necessary exemption, are outside this levy." From this passage, however, it is not possible to say whether exemption was granted to someone with less than, say, two talents in property or to anyone not registered among, e.g., the one thousand richest citizens. On the other hand, Aristotle (*Ath. Pol.* 56) shows two ways of avoiding a liturgy, filing a *skepsis* or demanding an exchange of properties (*antidosis*). He does not list insufficient property as a ground for *skepsis*, but then we cannot be sure that his list of grounds is complete. Still, I suggest that the remedy for insufficient property was *antidosis* rather than *skepsis*. That is, it does not matter whether I have slightly more or slightly less than an absolute minimum. What counts is, whether someone else has more. If so, I will challenge him to undertake the liturgy or exchange his property for mine.

forward course, his hearers could have distinguished the inherited property of Stratocles from his acquisitions, and it would have been necessary to explain with more clearness the way in which Stratocles was enriched by the adoption of his daughter." This particular criticism, however, is ill founded, for, as we have noted, Theopompos himself did not know precisely how Stratokles was able to accumulate his fortune. Nor would Isaeus choose Wyse's course, for artistic purposes. To prescribe the components of the original inheritance would involve the same sort of superfluous detail that Sositheos insists on bringing in and would detract from Isaeus' main tactic, the lengthy recital of Stratokles' holdings and the brief tale of Theopompos' property.

Still, there is one point here which engenders mistrust. Theopompos claims to have an estate of one talent, one thousand drachmai (apart from the estates of Hagnias and Makartatos). Yet it appears that it would take a net worth of at least two talents to put someone into the group of wealthiest citizens liable for liturgies.[76] Why define his estate at less than two talents, when he could simply say "a one talent estate," ταλαντιαῖος? The answer may be that the brothers actually inherited about two talents each, and he was hard pressed to explain the discrepancy. Either he kept some of his wealth in cash and refused to declare it, as his adversaries allege, or else he was a wastrel. In either event, he would want to cover his tracks. This method would avoid a flat lie.

On the other hand, I would not fault Isaeus' use of an argument from probability to establish the size of their patrimony, for he had no alternative if, as I suggest, Theopompos was the only one still alive who had intimate knowledge of Charidemos' estate. Although Wyse points out that "rich men sometimes married poor girls," an argument from probability is concerned with what usually happens, not what invariably happens. And, in fact, allusions in other speeches and a large number of boundary stones confirm Theopompos' statement that a dowry of twenty mina is a modest one.[77]

41. The ms. twice calls Stratokles' brother-in-law "Theophron" and once "Theophon".[78] Since both are Athenian names, it is not

[76] Cf. Dem. 27.64.

[77] Cf. Wyse, 243, and Moses I. Finley, *Studies in Land and Credit in Ancient Athens, 500-200 B.C. The Horos Inscriptions* (New Brunswick), 175.

[78] When its descendants offer "Theophon" instead of "Theophron", I take it that they are aiming at uniformity and have no independent value.

possible to decide between them. For convenience, I have called him by the latter name. Nor do we know his deme or any possible blood relationship with Stratokles. Just why he adopted a daughter instead of a son is beyond our ken. As we saw earlier (on § 8), this speech has two of the three instances of such an adoption that we know of. His property and position as one of the ten tribal commanders of cavalry place him in the landed gentry.

The fact that Theopompos assigns a value to this estate but does not specify its income suggests to me that the girl is now married and her husband in control of the property. Theopompos would then be unable to learn its earning power but still would have access to the record of her property that must have been kept in case of a divorce. The suspicious will say that Theopompos suppresses the income from the estate because it would show that the legacy was worth much less than two and one-half talents.

Whatever the true worth, Theopompos naturally uses figures which would seem plausible to the jury. Although two talents is a high price for a farm, one located in the rich Thriasian plain, some ten miles west of Athens, might fetch that amount. Two thousand drachmai would be a fair valuation of a flock of this size, for in various inscriptions which regulate methods of sacrifice we find that goats and sheep must normally be worth between ten and fifteen drachmai each to be acceptable, while a fine horse might be worth about one thousand drachmai.[79]

42. Theopompos probably had access to documents proving the cost of the houses which Stratokles bought, the amount of loans outstanding, and the estate's income. The fact that he can only estimate the value of the farm might suggest that Stratokles inherited it, but the estimate is so out of proportion to the worth which Theopompos assigns to his own farm (§ 44) that I prefer to believe that Stratokles purchased this property with the money he earned from his daughter's legacy.[80] Theopompos, then, refused

[79] On the worth of the farms and animals cf. W. K. Pritchett, "The Attic Stelai, Part II," Hesperia 25 (1956), 258-260, 270-273; for ἵππος λαμπρός as a technical term of uncertain meaning cf. J. K. Anderson, *Ancient Greek Horsemanship* (Berkeley, 1961), 122-123.

[80] It is also difficult to see what else he could have done with this money. As I visualize the situation, Stratokles purchased the land at Thria because of its proximity to the farm at Eleusis. That way he could manage both estates easily, having a house nearby and another in Athens (on the hill west of the Agora). He must have leased slaves to work the land.

to accept the purchase price as an adequate measure of its true worth. In either case he has reached his valuation of the property by capitalizing its income by a factor of twelve, making it the most valuable single piece of land mentioned in the orators or Attic inscriptions.[81] Although this must make us suspicious, we do not have enough evidence to determine whether this capitalization rate is reasonable.[82] There is nothing exceptional, however, about his treatment of the houses and loans.[83]

The entire estate, as Theopompos describes it, running to five and one-half talents, is the second largest to appear in the speeches of Isaeus but is certainly not out of line with some of the others (three to five talents),[84] and is certainly not one of the few enormous fortunes that such men as Nikias and Pasion owned.[85] The ward's income was about three times that of a skilled workman.[86]

I propose to take Isaeus literally when he writes that Stratokles left loans outstanding which bring in so much. That is, Stratokles made these loans himself, and they are still outstanding. But, of the leases he says only that they are bringing in money, he does not say whether Stratokles or the guardians granted them. The produce in the next section virtually proves that Stratokles was engaged in farming. If he was working the land at Thria, it must have been the guardians who leased it after his death. We have already seen (on section 34) that the archon could hold a public auction to lease an orphan's property. However, it is very likely that the archon let estates in their entirety,[87] while Stratokles' holdings were clearly

---

[81] Cf. Pritchett, *loc. cit.*, 270-273; Finley, *op. cit.*, 172-175. For the likelihood that the inscriptions tabulated by Finley seriously understate the value of the land cf. V. N. Andreyev, "Some Aspects of Agrarian Conditions in Attica in the Fifth to Third Centuries B. C.," Eirene 12 (1974), 12-13, and John V. A. Fine, *Horoi. Studies in Mortgage, Real Security, and Land Tenure in Ancient Athens* (Hesperia, Supplement 9, 1951), 140.

[82] Gustav Billeter, *Geschichte des Zinsfusses im griechisch-römischen Altertum bis auf Justinian* (Leipzig, 1898), 10-18, gives the evidence we have, but it is not possible to generalize from a few instances; cf. also Diederich Behrend, *Attische Pachturkunden* (Munich, 1970), 80-83, 118-119.

[83] Theopompos means that nine obols are due on each one hundred drachmai of principal *monthly*, an annual rate of eighteen per cent, which would be reasonable for loans carrying some risk; cf. Billeter, *op. cit.*, 18-29.

[84] Cf. Wevers, *op. cit.*, 96-97.

[85] Xenophon *Poroi* 4.14-15; Demosthenes 36.5.

[86] The craftsmen working on the buildings at Eleusis during this period received two to two and one-half drachmai per day. (*I.G.* II^2 1672-1673) We can probably allow three hundred working days a year at the most.

[87] Finley, *op. cit.*, 40-41. In § 34 Theopompos presumes that his ward's share of Hagnias' estate would be leased as a unit.

hired out piecemeal. The guardians, then, selected the lessees themselves, as was their right.

43. An ἔρανος is an interest-free loan granted by a group of men to accommodate a friend or client. The contributors sometimes chose a treasurer to manage the arrangement. Since the normal meaning of ὀφλήματα is "fines", it appears that the lenders went to court to recover the monies which they had advanced and that the defendant (or defendants) had paid part or all of the fine levied against him. The exact nature of this repayment cannot be determined with any certainty. My approach is to consider once again how Theopompos has acquired his information. As guardian of the girl, he knows the extent of her inheritance and can prove it; likewise as guardian of the boy, he is in a position to know and prove his inheritance. But he clearly implies that his only evidence for the one thousand drachmai in fines is the mother's registration statement. Thus I do not think that she filed with the archon an inventory of her husband's entire estate, including these fines. Instead, she listed them separately, in some other transaction. It was she and not her legal representative who did so, because she lacked documentary proof and had to give personal knowledge of her husband's affairs. (A plausible reason for this would be that the agreement between lenders and borrower was deposited with a third party or with the treasurer of the loan fund.) Moreover, instead of appealing to a public magistrate, she may have made representations directly to the borrower or the treasurer. Following a suggestion by Wyse, we might imagine that she asserted that her husband had received only one thousand drachmai out of a larger sum owing to him and demanded the remainder. If so, however, Isaeus let slip the opportunity to credit Stratokles' estate with both the sums collected and those still outstanding. Thus it seems more likely that the treasurer had exacted the fines from the defendant but had not yet distributed the funds among the contributors. The mother asked him for Stratokles' share, about one thousand drachmai. Theopompos himself was not involved in this business. Either he had not yet become the boy's guardian, or the mother was not on good terms with him. She must have been assisted by the other guardian or one of her own relatives.

Theopompos probably returned to this point later in the speech, when he took up the property which his opponents had hidden from view, and maintained that the treasurer paid over the one thousand drachmai to the boy's mother or the other guardian and that they are now concealing it. If they chose to answer such an allegation, they might deny that the treasurer paid the monies due or say that they belong to the mother as part of her dowry.

44. The farm at Oinoe was probably inherited from Theopompos' father; the one at Prospalta belongs to his son, whom he installed as the heir of his brother-in-law, Makartatos, by posthumous adoption. Prospalta lay at the south end of the rolling eastern plain of Attica, the Mesogeia, and was the ancestral deme of Makartatos' family. We do not know which of the two demes named Oinoe is meant here; one was near Marathon, the other far to the west, near the border with Thebes. In either case Theopompos' property was very remote from Athens.

Just how much Hagnias' estate was really worth, we have no idea. Notice that Theopompos does not magnify its importance by enumerating the properties or monies of which it consisted.[88] Nor, of course, does he itemize the animals or buildings of his farms, nor tell the jury the income of his possessions. The object is not to conceal, but simply to oppose as few discrete units as possible against as many as possible in the boy's estate.

45-46. Once again Theopompos presents himself as an accommodating and reasonable person, adding all his own family's property together, but reckoning the opposition's possessions separately. Actually, of course, he manages to get across the total value of their property. As we noted, since Theopompos describes the estate as worth two and one-half talents when Stratokles acquired control and as worth the same now, it would appear that Stratokles enjoyed the usufruct. The alternative is to suppose that it was originally less valuable but that (to put it charitably) for simplicity's sake Isaeus did not bother to mention and explain the increase. Naturally, if faced with a choice of naming the greater or lesser value, he would mention the greater.

In order to bring a charge of false witness, a litigant was required to make a complaint (ἐπίσκηψις) during the trial at which the perjury was allegedly committed.[89] He probably also had to file a suit against the offender in the usual manner. In any event, we hear of men who lodged an *episkepsis* but did not actually bring

---

88 From Sositheos' speech (69-70) we learn that it included a large olive grove at Araphen on the east coast of Attica.

89 Cf. Harrison, II, 192-197.

the case to trial. Since Theopompos must have produced witnesses to discredit the elder Phylomache's parentage, we should expect that it was Sositheos who filed the complaint. It is hard to find any issues of fact, rather than law, which could exist between Theopompos and Hagnias' mother and brothers.

I see no real reason not to take Theopompos literally when he says that, if any witness was convicted, the case had to be reheard.[90] His phraseology is entirely in line with that found in Attic inscriptions, such as the Eleusinian First Fruits Decree: ἐὰν δέ τις παραβαίνει τούτον τι, ἀποτινέτο πεντακοσίας δραχμάς (if anyone contravenes any of this, let him pay five hundred drachmai).[91] He appears to be paraphrasing the perjury law fairly closely. Some scholars object to Isaeus' formulation of the law on the *a priori* ground that it would permit a judgement to be overturned by conviction for a minor or irrelevant falsehood. But this founders on the problem of how to decide what is irrelevant or minor. Today a panel of judges would review the transcript of the trial to determine this question, but the Athenians had neither transcripts nor a Supreme Court. The only practical way would be to stay the previous verdict and to rehear all the evidence, i.e., to have a new trial, just as Isaeus indicates.

Theopompos had a little to gain from lying on this point, but not much. It was to his advantage to exaggerate the precariousness of his tenure, but I think that the jury was well aware that, with trials for perjury pending, his possession was not secure, regardless of the exact details of the procedure for invalidating previous decisions.

It seems very strange to me that after spending so much effort to convince the jury that he came into possession of Hagnias' estate

[90] I cannot understand how Harrison, II, 194, n. 2., can approve Lipsius' treatment (*op. cit.*, 958, n. 11) of ἐὰν ἁλῷ τις τῶν ψευδομαρτυρίων: "Aber im Sinne von εἷς kann τὶς am wenigsten da stehen, wo mehrere Zeugnisklagen erwähnt sind." It is Isaeus who speaks of multiple trials; the law is the same whether one or more witnesses is challenged: if anyone is convicted, the process begins anew. For the strategic value of bringing multiple suits cf. George Miller Calhoun, "'Επίσκηψις and the Δίκη Ψευδομαρτυρίων," C. P. 11 (1916), 390-391. Plato in the *Laws* (937C-D) requires that a majority of the depositions be convicted, but there are considerable discrepancies between his handling of perjury and the official Athenian procedure; cf. Glenn R. Morrow, *Plato's Cretan City* (Princeton, 1960), 287.

[91] *I.G.* I^2 76, lines 57-58; for other examples cf. Wilhelm Larfeld, *Handbuch der griechischen Epigraphik*, II (Leipzig, 1902), 693-695.

in a perfectly legitimate way and without any conniving on his own part, Theopompos now casts doubt on that legitimacy by mentioning the possibility of perjury. What makes it worse is that he earlier (25) tried to maintain that he had no need of witnesses in his contest with Phylomache.

47. Once again, complaints of audacity, slander, and lying, this time in connection with the opponent's accusation that Theopompos has hidden much of his wealth to escape taxes. This common charge is based on the fact that Athens taxed capital rather than income, so that by converting land into cash it was easier to escape detection. Everyone could see your land, but no one could keep track of your cash or investments. Whether Theopompos pays his taxes or not is irrelevant to the main issue of the case, but does go toward showing that he is the sort of person to defraud his nephew.[92]

48. The father of Chaireleos and Makartatos was Apolexis of Prospalta (Sos. 48), so that the farm of Chaireleos mentioned in the next section had probably been in the family for generations; where Makartatos' property lay, we do not know.

Apparently Athenian law recognized associations for collecting booty,[93] and most interpreters think that Makartatos may have been engaged in that pursuit. Presumably he intervened on behalf of one or more Cretan cities engaged in a war with Sparta and/or her island allies. A motive for his actions might have been to assist a guest-friend (*xenos*), although we might expect Isaeus to say so, if it were true. It would be pointless to say, "you are all witnesses," if many of the jurors were too young to remember Makartatos' exploits. "Many of you," "most of you," or "the elder among you" would have been as effective rhetorically. If we accept the validity of the deposition in section 31 of Sositheos' speech, the present trial took place soon after 361, so that Makartatos' foray belongs after the Common Peace of 371, which ended the seven-year Theban War between Athens and Sparta. Anyone who finds the Peace of Antalkidas a more suitable occasion for Athenian concern about provoking Sparta will have one more reason to jettison the deposition and date the trial to the 380's.[94]

---

[92] Cf. Isaeus 7.35 and Lysias 20.23.

[93] *Digest* 47.22.4.

[94] According to Harpokration (*s.vv.* Προσπάλτιοι and σιπύα), Lysias wrote a speech concerning a claim to half of the estate of a man named

Modern estimates place the cost of building a trireme as just under one talent, with the same amount needed to equip it.[95] However, Makartatos probably bought his used, at a greatly reduced price. In order to man the ship he would be required to pay a crew of two hundred at between one-half and one talent per month. Unless Cretan friends subsidized him, he must have intended to pay his men from the booty he would capture.

It is not unusual for a speaker to call upon the jurors as witnesses to a matter of common knowledge (or wide-spread prejudice). Aside from easing the burden of proof, this device establishes a bond between the speaker and the jury, who share this knowledge between them. In this particular case, though, Isaeus apparently goes far beyond legitimate bounds. Even though Makartatos' activities were talked about in public, could everyone be sure that he had sold all his possessions? And surely not everyone knew the extent of his brother's holdings. Presumably Theopompos could offer ordinary witnesses or documents to prove how much each of his brothers-in-law left. Still, his appeal to the jury as witnesses was not superfluous, for, as I said, it creates a common sympathy between them.

49. The farm at Prospalta passed from Chaireleos to Makartatos and then to their sister. Her husband had the use of it until their offspring were grown, when they would come into possession of it. From the case at hand we learn that the husband was obligated to include such a holding as part of his possessions for the purpose of calculating taxes.

The adopted son was named Makartatos. When Theopompos' other son died, Makartatos returned to his original family as Theopompos' heir. Athenian law allowed this if the adopted son had fathered a son to carry on the other line. Once Makartatos had inherited his father's property, he had to defend himself against Sositheos, whose presentation is now preserved as Ps.-Dem. 43.

As usual, the critics are skeptical of Theopompos' motives in allowing his son to be adopted as Makartatos' heir. Some think that his purpose was indeed to avoid paying taxes, but Davies suggests

---

Makarkatos, which mentioned the Prospaltioi. Since the accepted date for Lysias' death, c. 380, does not accord with our chronology, we can suppose that this Makartatos belonged to an earlier generation and was perhaps Apolexis' brother, or we can reject the attribution to Lysias.

95 Cf. C. H. Wilson, "Athenian military finances, 378/7 to the peace of 375," Athenaeum 48 (1970), 304-309; we can only infer naval wages from earlier conditions: cf. Thucydides 8.29 and 45; Xenophon *Hell.* 1.5.

that the adoption "was the only means of gaining a secure hold on a property on which someone else would otherwise have a better claim .... I would guess that either Chaireleos or Makartatos left an heir, who but for the [adoption] of Makartatos (II) would have inherited the estate of both brothers ...." [96] However, if Chaireleos had left an heir, his estate would never have passed to his brother; while the only heirs of Makartatos who could outrank his nephew would be lineal descendants, who surely could not be defeated by posthumous adoption. Moreover, although the speaker of Ps.-Dem. 44 certainly complains loudly enough about his opponents' tactics of using posthumous adoptions to block the aspirations of *collateral* heirs (*passim*), at no point does Sositheos tax Theopompos with cheating a lineal heir by his strategem. If there is anything to Davies' suggestion, it would be that a second sister of Makartatos, or someone purporting to be descended from her, claimed an equal share with the nephew of the deceased, Theopompos' son.[97] If the adoption could sustain a court challenge, it would serve to eliminate such a competitor.

If the adoption did gain Theopompos money, I am sure that he was glad of it, but I do not think that we should discount the reason he actually gives for it. Certainly the jury will have found it plausible, and in another speech Isaeus sums up the Athenian attitude toward dying without an heir: "All who are going to die take concern for themselves so that they may not leave their houses extinct but that there may be someone to sacrifice and perform all the customary rites for them. Wherefore, even if they die childless, still at least they adopt and leave someone." (7.30) I do not see how even the most cynical can doubt that Makartatos' sister was genuinely concerned to provide him an heir, nor can anyone who has read Lysias' description (32.11-18) of how Diogeiton's daughter fought for her children against her father fail to appreciate the power of the Athenian woman in family matters.

50. The other guardian argues that by obtaining the farm at Prospalta Theopompos would move from the class of ordinary tax payers to the liturgical class. If there was a minimum qualification for inclusion in this group, there would be a straight-forward way

---

[96] *Op. cit.*, 86.

[97] This would account for the title of the speech attributed to Lysias. On the equal shares accruing to the deceased's aunt and nephew see Isaeus 7.19.

to refute the charge: simply add the value of the two estates together to prove that they do not meet the minimum. But if, as I believe, liturgies were assigned on the basis of one's relative wealth, it would be difficult to refute this charge, if the total property was substantial. Consequently, Isaeus may have resorted to subterfuge. Originally Theopompos was not subject to liturgies, but once in control of Hagnias' estate, he certainly was. He has not been in this position long enough, though, to have performed enough services to bother enumerating them. What is really at stake is the order in which he acquired his two additional legacies. If he obtained Hagnias' estate first, the addition of Makartatos' property would make no difference to his tax status. But if he initially added Makartatos' estate to his own patrimony, the total of the two (a *minimum* of one and two-thirds talents) might have put him close to liturgical status. Thus, even though he later had to perform one or two liturgies, *at that earlier time* it might have been possible for him to avoid them by arranging the adoption. If, in fact, his motive for permitting the adoption was proper, as he says it was, this would be a classic case of having to use a false argument to refute a false charge, as lawyers and politicians sometimes must.[98]

The pooling of interests which Theopompos suggests is similar in spirit to the Athenian institution of *antidosis*.[99] When someone was called upon to perform a liturgy and felt that another was better able financially to do so, he could challenge him to exchange their original property and then with his new estate he would discharge the original obligation. The problem in this procedure and in Theopompos' challenge as well is that either party could hide his money and investments, so that only land, houses, slaves, and cattle would be exchanged or shared. The ward probably knew very well that his land and buildings were worth more than his uncle's and, of course, would refuse the redivision, since he could have no hope of getting his share of Theopompos' cash, whatever it was. Logically, Theopompos is begging the question. If the jury accepts his version of how much money the two sides have hidden, it will approve his challenge. But that version needs to be proven, not

---

[98] On my view, Wyse's opinion that Isaeus uses ἐλῃτούργουν in the non-technical sense of, "I performed my (ordinary) civic duties," is inapposite, as is the rejoinder by Naphtali Lewis, "Pro Isaeo, II, 50," A. J. P. 80 (1959), 162-168.

[99] Cf. Harrison, II, 236-238.

automatically granted credence. Thus, the speech breaks off with Isaeus trying to solve an impossible problem, trying to prove a negative. He can no more prove that Theopompos has no money hidden away than a modern politician, businessman, labor leader, or gangster can prove that he does not have a numbered Swiss bank account. Consequently, the orator must fall back on the hollow trick of the *petitio principii*.

In the rest of the speech I suggest that Isaeus relied primarily on the argument based on character, contrasting Theopompos' efforts to augment his ward's holdings with the other guardian's desire to obtain complete control of the property in order to pillage it. He also had the opportunity to go on the offensive again, both in making the prosecutor seem to be the defendant and in having Theopompos recount all the services he performed for the boy in managing his estate.[100]

The Verdict. Since Sositheos does not allude to these proceedings at all, it is clear that Theopompos emerged victorious. He also withstood the accusations of perjury against his witnesses, if they were actually brought to trial. Certainly, then, the juries in these various cases did not believe that the elder Phylomache was Polemon's full sister, as Sositheos alleged, or that Theopompos had agreed to divide his winnings with his brother or nephew. The result was that Theopompos retained Hagnias' estate until his death.

When Theopompos finally died, Makartatos returned to his original family as his heir, enrolling in the deme Oion and in the ancestral phratry of the Bouselidai. He left behind his own boy to take his place as son and heir of Makartatos of Prospalta. Sositheos then renewed his attempts to win Hagnias' estate.

---

[100] In § 44 Theopompos says that he will discuss later the money which the opposition has stolen away. Not only will this magnify the size of the ward's estate, it will give Theopompos a chance to expand on his thesis that the other guardian is the real criminal.

PART TWO

PS.-DEM. 43: MAIN DIVISIONS OF THE SPEECH

§§	
1-2	Introduction
3-17	Narrative
	Proof I, pragmatic
18-30	a. genealogy of the Bouselidai
	b. depositions, with comments
31-34	1. previous trials
35-41	2. Phylomache I's parentage
42-46	3. Euboulides II's position
47-50	c. *anakrisis*
51-52	d. the inheritance law
	Proof II, ethical
53-66	a. rights and responsibilities go together
	b. attitudes of the two families
67-72	1. Theopompos and Makartatos
73-75	2. Sositheos
76-80	3. Theopompos and Makartatos
81-84	4. Sositheos (Peroration)

SOSITHEOS' SPEECH
(Ps.-Dem. 43)

An inscription from the year 324/3 shows a certain Hagnias, son of Makartatos, of the deme Oion undergoing military training as a member of the ephebic corps.[1] Since the ephebes were eighteen and nineteen years old, this young man was born about 342. Since Sositheos (48, 76-77) makes much of the fact that none of the names in Hagnias' family appears in the house of Theopompos and Makartatos, we can probably date the proceedings around 345,[2] some fifteen years after Theopompos wrested Hagnias' estate from Phylomache and defended it against his nephew.

After Theopompos died, Sositheos had five years in which to challenge his heir's right to Hagnias' property, according to the law he cites at § 16. In that period he recruited some witnesses to his wife's ancestry and hired a competent speech writer.[3] As I see it, his advocate was faced with two disadvantages. Despite the fact that the trial is a *diadikasia* (a suit to determine the better claim, without a prosecutor or defendant), the parties were certainly not on an equal footing. Sositheos had to take the estate away from Makartatos and so must show that his claim was not based on a legal fiction or technicality. Nor could it be minimally better than Makartatos' claim: Sositheos had to have substantive reasons for taking the estate from its possessor. He could not win on a quibble. Secondly, his writer was going to have an extremely difficult time in establishing the factual basis of his case, namely, that the elder Phylomache was Polemon's full sister. The woman,

---

[1] Originally published by B. Leonardos, Ἀρχ. Ἐφ. (1918), 73-100; reprinted and interpreted by O. W. Reinmuth, *The Ephebic Inscriptions of the Fourth Century B. C.* (Mnemosyne, Supplement 14, Leiden, 1971), 58-82.

[2] Friedrich Blass, *Die attische Beredsamkeit*, III, 1 (Leipzig, 1893), 557-562, notes remarkable similarities between Sositheos' speech and Ps.-Dem. 48, which can be dated on internal grounds c. 340. It does seem likely that the two were written by the same man at about the same time.

[3] Blass, *op. cit.*, III, 1, 554-556, lists the arguments against Demosthenes as the author. Most are subjective or depend on the erroneous assumption that the writer has ruined a perfectly good case by his ineptness. The strongest point against Demosthenes' authorship seems to be the fact that this speech and Ps.-Dem. 48 share many turns of phrase not found in the rest of the Demosthenic corpus. Dionysius of Halicarnassus (*Demosthenes* 13) treats both speeches as products of the master.

after all, had been born a century earlier, so that the best Sositheos could do was to offer hearsay testimony at third and fourth hand. Faced, then, with these two problems, his speech writer adopted a single strategy to solve both. De-emphasizing the legal and factual elements of the case, he concentrates on an argument from equity: Sositheos and his family have performed all the duties of kinship toward Hagnias; Theopompos and Makartatos, none. Not only is Sositheos' side legally entitled to the inheritance, they *deserve* it. The other side does not. In this way he provides a strong motive for the jury to transfer ownership of the property, and by concentrating on the *logical* connection between rights and duties, he draws their attention away from the factual element, which is the weak point in his case.

1. At the very beginning of the speech Sositheos shows his determination to make the issue one of morality and not one of law. For Greek speakers naturally prefer to emphasize the area of their greatest strength and to ignore as far as possible their weak spots. Since Sositheos has little chance of proving his legal contentions, he resorts later in the speech to contrasting the behaviour of his family toward the deceased with the indifference shown by his rivals. Here, however, he confines himself to the negative aspect and immediately pins on them the label he intends they shall wear throughout the trial. For the first of several times he calls them lawbreakers and violent men. (Cf. §§ 23, 28, 68, 71, and 78.)

The earlier trials are Phylomache's suit against Glaukon, in which Theopompos appeared as a witness, Theopompos' own successful suit against Phylomache, and probably a charge of perjury brought by Sositheos against some of Theopompos' witnesses at the second trial.

2. After expanding his characterization of the opposition (they are also evildoers), Sositheos finishes his introduction in typical fashion, asking for a fair hearing and promising to be clear. (If the fairness accorded him was in proportion to his clarity, he was in trouble.)

3-4. According to the deposition in section 31 the date of Phylomache's victory is 361, but some scholars reject this as requiring too long a delay in the court proceedings following Hagnias' death c. 396. See further my comments on Isaeus, § 9.

As far as we know, the only contestant in the first trial was the possessor of the estate, Hagnias' half-brother Glaukon. Sositheos is surely going too far in saying that everyone admitted Phylomache's priority; at the most, they simply did not bother to deny it,[4] for Glaukon's entire claim rested on Hagnias' supposed will and he did not base his case on denying Phylomache's assertion that she was Hagnias' first cousin once removed. There is no reason to doubt that Theopompos testified on Glaukon's behalf, because he accepts the genuineness of the will in his own speech (8), but we do not know whether he testified simply that Hagnias did make a will or whether he described its contents in Glaukon's favor. At any rate, although he does not charge Theopompos with perjury, Sositheos manages to link him to sordid dealings. Naturally, Theopompos did not tell the jury of his own connection with Glaukon's defeat.

As we have noted before (on Isaeus 9), we have no way of telling why the jury rejected the will, but one point should be made here. To put it in modern terms, if the burden of proof fell in this instance on a man presenting a will in his own favor after a lapse of several years, the jury's vote against Glaukon would not necessarily mean that they considered the will a forgery, merely that they were not satisfied with the case he made for it.

Sositheos does not mention Hagnias' adopted daughter or tell the jury that Glaukos and Glaukon were Hagnias' brothers, for that would damage his claim to familial piety.

5. Since we have no other reference to a herald's proclamation as part of the process of claiming an inheritance, it is not possible to be sure at what stage it took place. (Cf. the commentary on Isaeus 9.) If it occurred before or during the trial involving Glaukon, Theopompos would naturally not enter a claim. Perhaps, though, the proclamation followed the jury's vote in Phylomache's favor and called for additional challenges before she could enter into possession of the inheritance. If so, Sositheos' point would have more effect on the jury. On reflection, however, one will realize that Theopompos was certainly right to postpone his claim until he could prepare an adequate case. If he had acted prematurely,

---

[4] Sositheos may be using ἀντομόσαι as a technical term, meaning that no one challenged Phylomache's paternity in the formal oaths taken at the preliminary hearing, but I take it in a wider sense: no one denied it at any time; cf. Wyse, 294.

he would have lost both the estate and his required deposit of one-tenth its value.

6. Apparently Phylomache defeated only one contestant, Glaukon, but from Sositheos' point of view, Glaukon, Glaukos, and Theopompos were all his opponents in that trial. Here for the first of many times he uses the initial verdict as one of his main strengths and can take Theopompos' refusal to abide by it as proof of his lawlessness. But, of course, in challenging that decision, Theopompos was merely exercising his rights, and the fact that he was successful should—logically—weigh more heavily than the first decision. Still, this prior victory does give Sositheos something to counter Makartatos' appeal to the verdict in his father's favor.

7. This is our only reference to Medeios of Hagnous (a deme near Prospalta, the seat of Theopompos' wife's family) and Eupolemos. The mention of their very names lends verisimilitude to Sositheos' account, as detail normally does. It is quite true that Athenians deposited agreements with third parties,[5] but by the time of this trial Medeios was probably dead, so unavailable to confirm or deny the story. Some scholars think that Eupolemos was claiming for himself and invent ways of making him a relative of Hagnias, but in my opinion he was representing Hagnias' mother.[6] In any event, Theopompos' speech (17) makes it certain that Hagnias' mother contested Phylomache's claim, a fact which Sositheos must suppress, for it was probably the strongest proof that the elder Phylomache was not the deceased's aunt. It is difficult to say why Sositheos calls Glaukos the defeated one rather than Glaukon, who was actually the one deprived of the estate. Perhaps he views him as the mastermind behind the plot. This would especially make sense if Glaukos was the father of the original heir, Hagnias' adopted daughter. Or again, if the trial took place shortly after Hagnias' death instead of thirty-five years later, Glaukos could be his brother's guardian and legal representative.

Phylomache succeeded in obtaining possession of Hagnias' estate by breaking the will, but the law (cf. § 16) still allowed challenges to her title by closer relatives. It is certainly easy to believe that Theopompos and the brothers cooperated. Perhaps

---

[5] Cf., e.gg., Isaeus 6.27 and Ps.-Dem. 48.11.

[6] Davies, *op. cit.*, 82-83; Broadbent, 96-97; see also *supra*, on Isaeus 16 and *infra*, on 10.

Glaukos and Glaukon went along in return for Theopompos' help at the first trial, or perhaps they still had hope of winning themselves. In either case, they had the same need to find witnesses to cast doubts on the birth of Phylomache's grandmother, the link between her and Hagnias. Theopompos says that Stratios and Stratokles were preparing to enter the contest, and his fellow guardian confirms that Stratokles was part of the coalition.[7]

8-9. Since an *amphora* contained twelve *choes*, the second speech allowed each contestant was one-fourth as long as the first. It is difficult for me to believe that the multiplicity of claims was *designed* to monopolize the speaking time,[8] although this certainly was one result, and we can sympathize with Sositheos on being outnumbered four to one (and with the jurors for having to listen to ten such speeches).

Previously Theopompos and the brothers had agreed on the genuineness of the will, but that was no longer the issue. The main point of agreement now is that the elder Phylomache was not the full sister of Polemon.

10. As we have seen before (on Isaeus 16), the jurors deposited their votes in urns devoted to each of the contestants. Three of the four urns were for Theopompos, Phylomache, and Hagnias' mother. Either Glaukon and Glaukos spoke on her behalf, and Eupolemos for himself, or, as I believe, Eupolemos represented the mother and the brothers filed identical claims and shared the same urn. It seems unlikely that a contestant could secure the advantage of double time by having two representatives, so that I judge that Eupolemos was the woman's third husband or was filling in for her proper legal representatives, her sons, who had their own case to present.

10-11. It is interesting to see how Sositheos crosses dangerous ground, disagreeing with the verdict without offending the jury. To do so, he must make excuses for the earlier jurors: it was only reasonable under the circumstances that they should be deceived, and he disguises what must have been his true feelings of anger.[9]

---

[7] Cf. Isaeus §§ 10 and 20. The trial took the form of a *diadikasia*, a process not to determine guilt or innocence, but to choose which claimant had the best right. Any number could participate.

[8] For my views on the actual reason cf. *supra*, on Isaeus 17.

[9] Cf. also Isaeus 5.8. Sometimes, however, speakers did dare to criticize the jury; cf. J. K. Dover, *Greek Popular Morality in the time of Plato and Aristotle* (Berkeley and Los Angeles, 1974), 23-25.

He shifts the blame for this miscarriage of justice to Theopompos, who plots, who contrives, who misleads. These (along with violence) are his standard accusations. And, of course, he tries to minimize his defeat by saying that the vote was close.[10] In reality, however, it went against him more heavily than he suggests, for any votes cast in favor of Hagnias' mother or brothers were votes to condemn Phylomache's pretensions.

We find several cases of posthumous adoption in the orators, including Makartatos' adoption as the son of his homonym, Theopompos' brother-in-law.[11] Although the intent was sometimes simply to secure an inheritance (Ps.-Dem. 44 furnishes notorious examples), on other occasions there must have been a genuine desire to perpetuate the line, for in one speech Isaeus is able to criticize his adversaries for failing to provide their brother with an heir by posthumous adoption. (7.31 and 44; cf. also 3.73) Yet in characteristic fashion Wyse (360) says that Sositheos "keeps out of sight the facts that he had four sons (§ 74) by the marriage, and notwithstanding waited more than 18 years before gratifying the alleged aspirations of the father of the ἐπίκληρος, and in the end merely acted in order to gain a pretext for reviving the dispute about the estate of Hagnias." In all fairness, however, the number of Sositheos' children is irrelevant, for he certainly does not represent his act as a sacrifice; there was no point in providing a child heir unable to perform the duties of the family cult, and we really do not know that he "merely acted in order to gain a pretext." It seems more likely, in fact, that Sositheos, prompted by his wife, did want to continue Euboulides' line.

In any event, the practical effect was to transfer Phylomache's entire claim to Hagnias' estate to the boy. In addition, he probably inherited all of Euboulides' own property. Some, however, have argued that even after this adoption Scsitheos' sons retained the right to share in Euboulides' estate, since Attic law provided that the sons of an *epikleros* were to obtain control of her father's property two years after coming of age.[12] Yet in default of decisive

[10] In Demosthenes 57 the speaker explains his defeat in the assembly of his deme by saying that his opponents delayed the vote until many members left and then stuffed the ballot box. (§§ 8-14)

[11] Isaeus 10.6 and 11.49; Ps.-Dem. 44, *passim*; for the motive see *supra*, on Isaeus 49.

[12] Ps.-Dem. 46.20; E. Hruza, *Die Ehebegründung nach attischem Rechte* (Erlangen and Leipzig, 1892), 91, n. 7., says that Sositheos' eldest son had

evidence, it seems much more natural to me to suppose that once Euboulides was given a son, Phylomache was no longer an *epikleros*, and thus her sons no longer entitled to inherit from their grandfather.

Virtually all Athenians belonged to a phratry, a religious and social organization based on descent. Some members of a phratry belonged to its various subdivisions, the *gene*. While they originally constituted an aristocracy or, at least, a privileged class of some sort, in the fourth century that was no longer true. Theopompos, Hagnias, and Euboulides inherited membership in their phratry from Bouselos; apparently they were not *gennetai*. "Introduction" among the phraters has three meanings: a man presented his new wife to them; he also showed them his new born children; and at the proper time, usually puberty, he proposed his sons for admission to the group.[13] (The regular occasion for these introductions was the Apatouria, the autumn festival of the phratries.) In addition, if a man adopted an adult, he would try to have him transferred to his own phratry.[14] Here we see the procedure followed when the adoption was posthumous, so that someone other than the new father acted as sponsor. It would seem that Sositheos waited until the boy reached puberty and then proposed him for admission to the phratry as the son of Euboulides. It was up to the phraters to accept or reject the candidate. (For the details of a similar, but more elaborate, process employed by another phratry or *genos*, cf. *I.G.* II² 1237 and the discussion by H. T. Wade-Gery, *Essays in Greek History* [Oxford, 1958], 116-134.)

The passage is important for the chronology of the case, for it seems to say that the boy was born after Theopompos' victory over Phylomache, which, following the deposition at 31, we place c. 359. If Sositheos did wait until the normal age for admission to the phratry and then filed suit, we have an interval of fifteen years or so, giving us a date of c. 345 for this trial, which agrees with the conclusion drawn in the introduction to this speech. One minor problem remains. According to our reconstruction of events, Phylomache came of age before 370, yet from section 73 we learn

come of age and was "nach dem Gesetze Herr seines Erbtheiles." However, we do not know that this son had fulfilled the statutory requirement of being *two years past* coming of age.

13 Some examples: Isaeus 3.76, 8.19, and 12.3; Demosthenes 57.54; Ps.-Dem. 59.59; Pollux 8.107.

14 Isaeus 2.14 and 7.15-17.

that this boy, named Euboulides, was her second or third surviving child. That implies a rather long delay between her puberty and his birth after 359.

12. Euboulides apparently instituted suit soon after Hagnias' death, challenging the will and claiming to be the nearest of kin through his mother, the elder Phylomache. (Cf. on § 43.) Sositheos is certainly at pains to connect Euboulides and Hagnias, for it is through Euboulides that he hopes to connect his son with the deceased. (Notice the fine touch in his reference to "their own family" rather than "his own," binding Euboulides and Hagnias even more closely.) As far as Euboulides' wishes are concerned, it is certainly true that Athenians normally preferred to adopt a close relative or a son-in-law, and in one of his speeches Isaeus speaks (3.73) of the likelihood that a dying man might leave his daughter as an *epikleros* and give instructions that one of the children born to her be adopted as his son.

Here we have for the first time reference to the "house of Hagnias," a key element in Sositheos' presentation. It normally means the house to which Hagnias II belongs, i.e., all the descendants of his grandfather Hagnias I, including Sositheos' wife and son.

13. As her father's only child, Phylomache was an *epikleros*, who could be claimed in marriage by his nearest relative. Sositheos vindicated his right to do so and thus acquired control of Euboulides' estate and management of his wife's claim to Hagnias' property. The couple were second cousins; cf. the commentary on 73. We have placed the marriage c. 370. Broadbent suggests that Sositheos intends the jury to think that he has established his right to marry Phylomache as the heiress of Hagnias rather than as her father's heiress. (80) That is not so clear in this passage, but it is certainly the case in section 20.

As I have said, Sositheos' strategy is to turn the issue into one of morality, to show that Theopompos and his son were only interested in Hagnias' money, while he and his family were concerned to carry out the duties of kinship toward the deceased. In this section he is able to present himself as pious indeed, arranging to fulfill the wishes of his father-in-law. Since Athenians normally did adopt a close relative, if adoption became necessary, the jury probably accepted Sositheos' version that Euboulides desired to have a grandson succeed him, and they would esteem Sositheos for making it possible. Unless Makartatos pointed it out, they also probably failed to recognize that Sositheos is taking credit for doing what he criticizes Theopompos for doing: each of them provided an heir for his wife's relative. Moreover, Sositheos has skilfully managed to confuse two separate issues, his piety toward Euboulides and his piety toward Hagnias, for it was only the former who sought an heir from Phylomache.

14. According to Sositheos, he proposed his son for adoption as Euboulides' son. Makartatos asked the phraters to oppose this course but was unwilling to perjure himself by interfering with the sacrifice. This is an extremely clever use of irrelevancy. Since the deme and the phratry were the basic units of Athenian society (after the family, of course), their members were in the best possible position to know of one's ancestors and to pass on one's legitimacy. Thus, if the phraters accept Sositheos' son, it would seem to be powerful support. However, all their vote really signifies is that they regard Phylomache as Euboulides' daughter and her son as legitimate. It says nothing about the central issue, the parentage of the first Phylomache. Sositheos, however, by constantly coupling Euboulides and Hagnias, tries to make it appear that the phraters recognized the boy as Hagnias' heir. Without this adoption Makartatos would have had no challengers to his possession of Hagnias' estate. Consequently, he would hope to prevent it, but he knew full well that he had no grounds for doing so. Euboulides was entitled to an heir, and certainly his grandson was the proper candidate. If, as Sositheos says, Makartatos suggested that the phraters should refuse to recognize the adoption, we can only guess that he charged that the whole thing was a subterfuge to gain Hagnias' estate rather than a *bona fide* continuation of Euboulides' line.

In his description of the sacred rite Sositheos achieves an impressive fullness and solemnity by repeating the article in such phrases as, "the phraters, those of Makartatos, the ones who know best," and by separating the subject from the verb with these articular phrases and with numerous participles including genitives absolute.

15. As a minor, the boy Euboulides had to be represented by an adult. After the adoption he was no longer related to his natural father but still retained his connection with his mother.[15] Thus

[15] Harrison, I, 93-94.

he is represented by her son, his elder brother Sosias. Nevertheless, Sositheos is permitted to "assist" Sosias, by speaking for him.

In introducing the law which authorizes this suit, Sositheos avoids the onus for prolonging this interminable case by pointing out that he is merely following his opponents' lead. At the same time he is able to remind the jury that one court at least had approved Phylomache's claim.

16. The award of an estate or an heiress in an *epidikasia* was not final, provided a new contestant came forth with a better claim. In fact, even one of the defeated parties could put forth a new claim, as Glaukon apparently did, filing as a half-brother after losing his case based on Hagnias' supposed will. (Cf. § 7.) This law indicates that an *epikleros* might be transferred from one husband to another, and Isaeus (3.64) says that it frequently happened. Scholars, however, are divided on the application of the statute.[16]

The deposit required to file a claim has figured prominently in both speeches, as the speakers tax their opponents with lacking the self-confidence to risk making a deposit and losing it.[17] Since the deposit would amount to one-tenth the value of Hagnias' estate, it would come to more than one thousand drachmai, a considerable sum. (Cf. Isaeus 44.)

According to Isaeus (3.58), "the law orders one to claim the estate within five years after the heir dies." This is the statute of limitations (προθεσμία) meant by the law here.[18]

Certainly the most important thing we learn from this quotation is the basis on which Makartatos must defend his possession. He does not have to show that he is Hagnias' closest relative; that would be impossible, for he is outside the *anchisteia* himself. Rather, he must show that Theopompos was entitled to inherit when he actually did so. Therefore, he will do exactly what his father did against Phylomache. He will demonstrate that Theopompos and Euboulides II were second cousins to Hagnias in the paternal line and that the latter's descendants, Phylomache and Euboulides III, are farther removed in the paternal line, and that Euboulides II and his descendants are not related to Hagnias at all in the

---

[16] Harrison, I, 309-311, summarizes the various views.

[17] Isaeus §§ 13, 15, and 27-28; Sositheos § 5.

[18] Cf. John F. Charles, *Statutes of Limitations at Athens* (Chicago, 1938), 55-59.

maternal line because Euboulides II's mother was not a legitimate full sister of Hagnias' father.

17. This is certainly a just request and the key to the whole case. If Sositheos can establish his wife's lineage, he is entitled to the inheritance.

3-17. This, then, is the conventional narrative, in which the speaker presents his version of the events leading up to the trial. In it Sositheos skilfully explains away his previous defeat and allays any suspicion that the boy's adoption was a callous trick to renew the litigation by presenting himself (as he does throughout the trial) as a man motivated only by family solidarity. He finishes by explaining how the case can be reopened and by alerting the jury to the factual issue at stake.

18-30. Now Sositheos turns to the traditional third section of a speech, the proof (or argument). I would construe this as having three subdivisions. In Aristotelian terms,[19] the second portion is a non-artistic proof, the presentation of (and insipid commentary on) the testimony of witnesses. In the third Sositheos argues that one cannot have the rights of an heir without at the same time having the duties, and that he and his family have performed those duties for Hagnias. Thus, he maintains that on the basis of his previous conduct his side is entitled to inherit. This is, I suggest, what Aristotle defines as a proof from character, an artistic proof, or one requiring skill. The first section (18-30) is also an artistic proof, in which Sositheos gives the details of the genealogy of the Bouselidai, interlarding his presentation with axiomatic arguments. The logic of his conclusions is, of course, uncontestable, but their application to the particular case is the Q.E.D. An important element in this section is the blatant character assassination, charges of violence, conspiracy, lying, deceit, and general licentiousness against his many opponents.

18. Broadbent (80) makes the interesting suggestion that Sositheos intended to present a great amount of genealogical material but was dissuaded by his speech writer.

19. Bouselos or his father must have been living in the deme Oion, or at least owned property there, when Kleisthenes established his constitution in 508 and caused all citizens to register in demes. The site of Oion is disputed. Of the two demes so named

[19] *Rhetoric* 1375a-1377b.

we know that Bouselos' family belonged to Oion Kerameikon.[20] Most scholars have taken the name to mean that the deme was near the Kerameikos, the potters' quarter of Athens and its suburbs extending west from the city's walls past the Academy. But various inscriptions which group demes by geography indicate that Oion was located somewhere in the hilly country, ten to twenty miles north of Athens.[21] Perhaps the name means that it was situated near a deposit of clay.

Since it was possible for brothers to hold their inheritance in common,[22] Sositheos must specify what is essential for his argument, that the sons of Bouselos divided the property and formed new families. They were not patrilocal, but neolocal, in the sense that they lived by themselves and not with their father. Bouselos apparently did what Lear did, but probably with greater precautions, for Lysias assures the jury that one would not give up everything without retaining something for himself: "for all men wish to be cared for by their children while having money rather than, lacking it, to need them."[23] A Euboulides of Oion served as a treasurer of Athena in 441/0, a guarantee of considerable wealth.[24] He was probably the son of Bouselos mentioned here.

20. The three are Euboulides, Kleokritos, and Habron. Did they actually have descendants who ranked with Theopompos? Certainly Euboulides did, Menestheus son of Philagros (44-45), and on my reconstruction either Habron or Kleokritos had a son who married Phanostrate and begot Stratios II. (Cf. the commentary on § 42 and Isaeus 8.) Furthermore, either Habron or Kleokritos had a daughter named Oinanthe, who in turn had a son called Stratonides (36), but as his connection with the deceased was through a woman, he probably ranked below Theopompos. There were also offspring who even outranked Theopompos, such as Euboulides' sons Kallistratos and Euktemon (42-46 and 73). In any case, I take it that Sositheos is implying here, not that

---

[20] From the list of ephebes, Reinmuth, *op. cit.*, 58, we learn that Hagnias son of Makartatos of Oion belonged to the tribe Leontis, of which (according to Harpokration, s.v. Οἶον) Oion Kerameikon was a part.

[21] Cf. my article, "Notes on Attic Demes," Hesperia 39 (1970), 65.

[22] Cf. Harrison, I, 239-240, for examples and discussion.

[23] 19.37; for arrangements in one area of modern Greece cf. J. K. Campbell, *Honour, Family and Patronage* (Oxford, 1964), 79-88.

[24] Russell Meiggs and David Lewis, *A Selection of Greek Historical Inscriptions to the End of the Fifth Century B.C.* (Oxford, 1969), 150.

these second cousins failed to file claims because they were outside the *anchisteia*, but that they and the rest of the family recognized the position of the first Phylomache. After all, it will not profit him to show that Theopompos had no claim unless he can show that his own side does. His implication is false, however, for before the will was broken they may have refrained from claiming in the belief or supposition that it was genuine, and by the time Phylomache succeeded in overthrowing it, they may have been dead. For instance, the depositions at 43-45 say only that Euktemon and Menestheus forbore a claim at the *epidikasia* brought on by Euboulides II. Since this trial probably took place soon after Hagnias' death in or near 396, they may well have died before Phylomache's victory in 361. Moreover, in order to establish the recognition of Phylomache, he must suppress the fact that Hagnias' own mother filed a claim and so must have denied the pretensions of the woman who was supposedly her sister-in-law. I do not agree with those who find a contradiction between this section and Theopompos' version (10) that his brother Stratokles and Stratios II, also second cousins to Hagnias, were preparing to file suit against Phylomache but died before actually doing so. Rather I think that Sositheos is telling the truth, but not the whole truth.

One can also entirely agree with Broadbent (80) that Sositheos tries here to trick the jury about Phylomache's position as an heiress. The fact that no one else claimed her is irrelevant, since Sositheos' rights were based on his kinship to Euboulides II, not her kinship to Hagnias. She was heiress to her father, not to Hagnias. Indeed, Makartatos might well argue that the others did not claim her because they knew that she was not Hagnias' *epikleros*.

21. Sositheos' contention is that the descendants of Hagnias I form one house, those of Stratios I a separate one, so that Phylomache and her son are the only survivors in the former. Why make Hagnias the founder of the family rather than his father, Bouselos, or his son, Polemon?[25] Broadbent, for one, apparently finds considerable anthropological significance in Sositheos' presentation of what she calls his "*oikos* doctrine." (74-79) But to my mind the reason for Sositheos' tack is simple rather than profound. Hagnias I is the only common ancestor of his son and the deceased who is

---

[25] Since Athenian law permitted second cousins to inherit, it implicitly recognized the great-grandfather as the fountainhead.

not also a common ancestor of Theopompos. That way, the son is in, Theopompos is out.

It does not seem worthwhile to refute in detail Broadbent's treatment of this "*oikos* doctrine." Suffice it to say that it starts from the mistaken view that only kin within five degrees of the deceased could inherit. Thus she supposes that Theopompos inherited as Hagnias' first cousin once removed, through the latter's mother. But she is forced to admit that such an explanation is inadequate: "Sositheos avoids mentioning Hagnias' mother at all, and uses the *oikos* doctrine instead. Our knowledge must therefore be inadequate; or rather, the simple opposition between fifth degree through Hagnias' father and fifth degree through Hagnias' mother cannot cover all the relevant facts considered by the courts and by Sositheos and his rhetor." (75-76) Therefore, she offers the hypothesis that Theopompos added a second element to his claim, paternal connection with the deceased, or, as she puts it, descent (from Bouselos) is added to kinship. This leads her to see a "genuine legal problem," argued by Theopompos and Sositheos, "the relation between kinship and descent in collateral inheritance within the jurally limited kind of five degrees." (76) None of this is necessary or even likely. Merely recognize that second cousins were fully entitled to inherit and you will see that the issue is one of fact, not one of law, *viz.*, whether the elder Phylomache actually was the legitimate full sister of Polemon. Since Sositheos cannot prove this satisfactorily, he must resort to two other avenues of persuasion. One is the old standby, the argument based on character. The second is also familiar. If his wife's grandmother was what he claims she was, certain consequences follow. By harping on those consequences (his *oikos* doctrine), he keeps attention away from the *demonstrandum*, the premise, that Phylomache I was indeed Polemon's sister.

22. At Isaeus 8.33 the speaker asks the jury, which is nearer: a daughter or a brother? grandchildren or a brother?, and concludes that grandchildren are *certainly* nearer than a nephew. But both speakers assume what needs to be proven, in that case that his mother is Kiron's daughter, here that Phylomache was Hagnias' daughter. (For the name of Stratios' child see the commentary on 42 and Isaeus 8.)

23. Hagnias, as we have seen on Isaeus 8, was captured and killed by the Spartans when he went on a diplomatic mission c. 396.

24. For simplicity Sositheos might have omitted the relationship between Philagros and Phylomache, but he must have considered it more important to suggest that a close relative validated her position in the family by marrying her. (Hagnias and Euboulides were sons of Bouselos so that their children were first cousins; first cousin marriage was a frequent occurrence among the upper classes at Athens, as I have shown in Phoenix 21 [1967], 273-282.) Likewise, although the repetition of names and relationships makes this section so difficult to comprehend, they do at least serve to drive home the crucial point, that Phylomache was Polemon's sister.

The elder Hagnias must have predeceased his son, who then allegedly became Phylomache's legal representative (*kyrios*) and bestowed her in marriage. Since Makartatos probably denied this, it is interesting to see Sositheos mention the marriage unobtrusively in an expository context rather than call attention to it as one of his main proofs of Phylomache's position. This way he does not arouse the jury's suspicions by protesting too much.

In addition to Theopompos, Charidemos had a son named Stratokles, who is irrelevant to Sositheos' presentation.

25. Sositheos now alternates narrative with argument, giving first the details of the genealogy of the Bouselidai and then showing how his self-evident principles of nearer kinship are to be applied in this particular case. The elementary nature of this application reminds one of the way Theopompos (42-45) performed simple arithmetic for the jury's benefit. Proceeding step-by-step, then, was considered a more effective method than presenting the jurors with a long, detailed narrative.[26] Sositheos also makes good use of the logical conditional sentence to gain assent,[27] and his repetition of the question, "which is nearer?", is especially forceful.

26. Throughout his speech Sositheos uses πρὸς πατρός to mean, "on the deceased's father's side." As for the key phrase ἀνεψιοῦ παῖς, he never discusses what it means but instead likes to set up genealogical chains, so that it follows ἀνεψιός and appears to be simply a descriptive term, "child of a cousin."

While one might think that the reference to Phylomache as a homopatric and homometric sister is merely to make this Euclidean

[26] Also cf. Demosthenes 27.9-11 and 35-37.

[27] Cf. Theopompos' extensive use of it in §§ 24-26 and 33-34.

proof complete, it serves the additional purpose of reiterating the point which is vital to the speaker's case.

When Makartatos returned to his original family, he left his only son as heir to the first Makartatos. He had not yet fathered another child to carry on the line of Stratios and Theopompos, but someday he would.[28]

27. In fact, Theopompos did claim to be an ἀνεψιοῦ παῖς. This is the only place where Sositheos comes close to challenging Theopompos' use of the term, but I think that he shows his inability to argue against it. For rather than saying what an ἀνεψιοῦ παῖς is and what he is not, Sositheos has recourse to his irrelevant complaint that Theopompos and Makartatos belong to an entirely different house.

28. Surely Sositheos is right that the nearest relative is entitled to inherit, but the whole point is, who is the nearest relative?

29. We do not know whether Sositheos' opponents alleged that the elder Phylomache was illegitimate or simply that Hagnias was not her father at all. Certainly Theopompos did not claim to belong to Hagnias' house; if anything, he must have said that the descendants of Bouselos constituted a single family instead of the five which Sositheos distinguishes. But to judge from Isaeus' speech, he simply relied on the letter of the law without raising wider questions.

30. Theopompos did in fact offer witnesses, for he tells us (45) that his possession was not yet secure since trials for perjury were pending. In addition to lying on this point, Sositheos suppresses the fact that Phylomache II was opposed by Hagnias' own mother, who was in an excellent position to know whether the elder Phylomache was her sister-in-law or not.

Having proceeded in severely logical fashion to prove the obvious, Sositheos finishes this portion of his proof with a rhetorical flourish, appealing once again, as Theopompos was wont to do, to the judgement of a previous jury, and using four synonymous words (out of fourteen) to suggest a conspiracy against him.

19-30. Why is it that Sositheos spends much of his time belaboring the obvious, showing that the descendants of the first Hagnias are closer to the deceased than the descendants of Stratios? Some critics say that Sositheos is simply incompetent and verbose;

---

[28] For Hagnias son of Makartatos of Oion cf. Reinmuth, *op. cit.*, 58.

another view is that he has a novel view of kinship to propound. These criticisms are based on the assumption that he was in the right and Theopompos in the wrong. Reverse the position and see what results. Sositheos, or his speech writer, has actually done a skilful job of making the best of a bad case. The relevance of his discussion depends on the premise that Phylomache I is the legitimate daughter of Hagnias I, but this premise is so weak that he can do little to establish it. Instead he concentrates on the conclusions that can be drawn from it. In that way his reasoning process will seem irrefutable and fair to the jury, and he will focus their attention on his strong point, his conclusions, and away from his weak point, the premise.

31. Theopompos certainly did not dispute that Phylomache had once gained a victory, and Makartatos could dispose of this weak reed by saying that the first jury had been misled but when the truth was finally revealed the second jury was able to render a valid verdict.

We have already discussed whether the archonship of Nikophemos, 361/0, is a plausible date for Phylomache's triumph. (Cf. the commentary on Isaeus, section 9.) Here it remains to remark that Sositheos several times says that she won her case in the dikastery, but this deposition speaks instead of the arbitrator. It is possible, of course, to emend the text to say "dikastery" instead of "arbitrator", but the need for emendation supports the view that this document is spurious.

32-34. Phylomache originally succeeded by casting doubt on the validity of Hagnias' supposed will; she certainly did not have to meet a determined challenge to her own pretensions to be a descendant of Hagnias I. When Theopompos finally brought that challenge, Sositheos was unable to meet it. Characteristically, he resorts to name calling rather than proof: Phylomache won fairly, Theopompos by contrivance and deception. *Ipse dixit.*

This portion of the speech contains several other interesting rhetorical devices: the constant iteration of Phylomache's (and his son's) claim to be an ἀνεψιοῦ παῖς, the attempt to draw the jurors into active participation in the case, and another argument based on irrelevancy. Of course the boy had never been defeated in court; he had never been to court before. His claim was no better than his mother's. Actually, one might say that the contest was between the young Euboulides and Theopompos, not Makartatos, who was entitled by law to rely on his father's relationship to the deceased.

35-37. These *testimonia* are designed to make one point, that Phylomache was the one and only legitimate heir of Hagnias. Her grandmother Phylomache was the full sister of his father Polemon, and Polemon had no brother to outrank her. It is my opinion that these witnesses give the rest of their testimony in sections 42-46. The argument for this view will be found after the commentary on § 46.[29]

36. I agree with those scholars who think that the first witnesses in this section also testify at 44. If so, their lineage runs, Oinanthe-Stratonides-Straton-these witnesses, in that order. Oinanthe, as first cousin to Polemon, will be the daughter of Habron or Kleokritos, the sons of Bouselos. She must have married into a family using the names Straton and Stratonides, which means "son of Straton."[30] There is no indication of the identity or relationship of the second witness. As phrater and fellow demesman of (the younger) Hagnias and Euboulides, he must be descended from Bouselos through the male line in each generation.

37. The mss. give the adopter's name as Archilochos, but editors emend to make this witness identical with the one in 45, the son of Archimachos. I agree with this, but it is possible that the two are different. One of the female descendants of Bouselos may have married into a family that used names beginning Archi-. It was a frequent Greek practice to use a set of names having one of the two elements in common. Unfortunately, there is no indication of this man's (or these men's) place in the family.[31] If they are one, "Archimachos" would seem the *lectio difficilior*, as the scribe had his mind on poetry rather than *testimonia*. For two

[29] Broadbent's chart on 103 is based on the view that the two groups of deponents are distinct, and her dates of birth are based on the conclusion that this trial occurred in 375.

[30] A certain Stratonides son of Straton of Oion Kerameikon was an ephebe in 324/3; cf. Reinmuth, *op. cit.*, 58. He might be the son of one of these witnesses. If so, Oinanthe must have married a man from her own deme. However, this combination of names is so apt that it does not tax the imagination to suppose that many families used it.

[31] Broadbent, 101, notes that the first deposition in 37 "is by a relative of Polemon only among the Bouselids, and this may mean that he represents Phylomache I's mother's family," but Oinanthe is a Bouselid even though her only stated connection is with Polemon.

other examples of adoption by the maternal grandfather see Isaeus 10.4 and Ps.-Dem. 42.21 and 27.

Kallistratos was the son of Euboulides I and married a granddaughter of Habron; their daughter married Sosias and gave birth to Sositheos (73-74). If the text is correct, the witness' connection with Kallistratos is irrelevant since his testimony depends entirely on hearsay from his mother. We can only conclude that he is seeking to increase his authority by mentioning Kallistratos. If this man actually is his son-in-law, we must be on our guard, for Sositheos' father is also Kallistratos' son-in-law. Thus, this witness may very well be the complainant's own father. In my view, however, the text needs to be emended: the witness is the grandson of Kallistratos and perhaps Sositheos' brother. Inasmuch as this is part of my general interpretation of the depositions, I postpone my reasoning until after the commentary on section 46, where I also discuss the meaning of ἀνεψιοῦ παῖδα here.[32]

Broadbent says (101-102) that these documents represent "official opinion in the deme of Oion" (§ 35), "the special knowledge of the womenfolk of the Bouselids" (36A), "the agnatic Bouselid tradition—Phylomache's father's family" (36B), and the traditions of her mother's family (37A) and husband's family (37B). Although this would present a very impressive array of support for Sositheos' position, it would be characteristic of him not to make it clear to the jury. However, it does not make sense to me to speak of "the special knowledge of the womenfolk" or "the agnatic tradition" in a family which intermarried as much as this one. The 'special knowledge of the womenfolk' is, after all, passed on through three generations of men. Or take, as an example, Phanostratos or Phanostrate, the son or daughter of Stratios mentioned in sections 22 and 42. Can it make a whit of difference whether this person's descendants recited an agnatic version or cognatic version? In any case, there was no single agnatic version: Theopompos himself was an agnate. Sositheos did not have much leeway in the

[32] If the text is correct and, further, if the witness' mother is related to Polemon through Bouselos as his first cousin once removed, she will be the granddaughter of one of Bouselos' sons. Of course, she cannot be the granddaughter of Polemon's father and she is not likely to belong to Theopompos' branch of the family. She might be descended from Euboulides I through Euktemon, Kallistratos, or an unknown daughter, or again her grandfather might be either Kleokritos or Habron. Since Sositheos' mother was a great-granddaughter of Habron, this witness could be her brother.

selection of his witnesses; he could not afford to take representatives of various "traditions" within the family. At this late date in the proceedings he had to take anyone who was available to support his version.

Some scholars have concluded from the wording of these depositions that someone claimed to be a descendant of Polemon's *brother* and so entitled to inherit Hagnias' estate. However, I think that these depositions were prepared especially for this case, where no such claim was made, rather than left over from a previous encounter. I also think that Sositheos has carefully coached his witnesses to bring out the points that he wants made. He cannot afford to drag in a red herring, such as an actual claim to descent from the brother of Polemon; rather, he mentions the possibility of a brother simply to exclude it as part of a logically complete showing that only Phylomache and her son are left alive in the house of Hagnias.

38. It is hard to believe that Sositheos was unaware of his opponents' strategy—what alternative did they have but to challenge Phylomache's ancestry? And what recourse did he have but to solicit testimony from family members who supported his contention? Sositheos prefers to hide this with his conspiracy theory.

39. From this account we cannot tell what his opponents alleged about Phylomache's grandmother, for like most speakers Sositheos does not do justice to the opposition's position. Whatever they maintained, it must have seemed plausible, or Sositheos would have told us more about it in order to ridicule it. Although τὸ παράπαν may suggest that Phylomache I was called a complete imposter, the possibility remains that Theopompos and the others said that she was Hagnias' bastard or his wife's daughter by a previous husband.

40-41. It seems likely that most of Theopompos' witnesses and fellow claimants were dead by now, so that Makartatos would have a hard time reproducing the earlier testimony against the first Phylomache.

The recital of kin is an impressive *tour de force* and serves to remind the jury of the family tree, but only one relationship matters: was Phylomache Polemon's full sister?

Philagros and Euboulides were first cousins once removed, standing one generation apart. We know that ἀνεψιαδοῦς is the proper term to describe the younger member of such a pair. Here and in section 49 we have the only indication of the Attic term for the other member, *viz.*, ἀνεψιός, which otherwise means first cousin.

42-46. The point of sections 43-45 is to show that no one in the family opposed Euboulides' claim to Hagnias' inheritance. Section 42 shows why: although he was only one of several second cousins on his father's side, he was regarded as a *first cousin* on his mother's side. 44 and 45 are additionally concerned to explain how he outranked his brother. Menestheus' only claim to the inheritance was through his father, not his mother. The order of the depositions is based on their content rather than the relationship of the deponent.

42. There is no indication of this witness' identity. As I just said, the importance of his testimony is that it supports the contention that Euboulides ranked with Theopompos as a second cousin but ahead of him as a first cousin through the elder Phylomache. Euboulides' adopted son, then, would prevail over Theopompos and his son. To make his point completely he names all the children of the two uncles of Polemon who figure in the case, Euboulides and Stratios. As usual, Habron and Kleokritos and their offspring are ignored, just as Sositheos tells the jury they will be. (20-21)

The mss. here name "Phanostrate daughter of Stratios," but at § 22 some of them say that "Phanostrate," others that "Phanostratos," was born to Stratios. Editors emend section 42 to read, "Phanostratos father of Stratios," citing Theopompos' statement at § 8, "I, Hagnias, Euboulides, Stratokles, and Stratios, the brother of Hagnias' mother, are born from cousins. For our fathers are cousins (born) of uncles." They think that Stratios the younger is descended from his namesake through his father (Phanostratos), but in commenting on § 8 I explained that Stratios II could be descended from Stratios I through his mother (Phanostrate) *and* from one of Bouselos' other sons, Habron or Kleokritos, through his father. This only requires us to postulate another first cousin marriage in this family, and the corruption of "Phanostrate" to "Phanostratos" is much easier than the one which the editors assume. Moreover, since Sositheos mentions only one Stratios, the elder, any reference to "Phanostratos father of Stratios" would be unintelligible to the jury. (The younger is known only from Theopompos' speech.)

On the other hand, there is a mandatory correction to be made where the mss. call Kallistratos the father of Sositheos' wife. Since we learn from §§ 73-74 that Kallistratos is the father of *Sosias'* wife, the mother of Sositheos, we must write either "Sosias' wife" or "Sositheos' mother" here.

Euktemon is the son of the first Euboulides. The next witnesses (43) refer to him as Philagros' homopatric brother, but I doubt that we should infer that he had a different mother. The point of this testimony is to emphasize that, although he had a claim, Euktemon did not press it. Since the claim is through his father, the witnesses stress that Euktemon was Philagros' homopatric brother without implying anything about his mother. Euktemon was a first cousin once removed to Hagnias and so outranked Euboulides in the paternal line; the suggestion is that he yielded to Euboulides as a first cousin in the maternal line. Again, I doubt that we should infer that Euktemon had any children; when the witness says here that Euboulides ranked with "the sons of them and Hagnias," he does not necessarily mean with "the sons of each and every one of them." He may simply mean with "the sons of those who had sons."[33] Euktemon filled the important office of *archon basileus*, who managed virtually all the ancestral religious festivals and most murder trials. (Cf. *Ath. Pol.* 57.)

43. As we have noticed (on Isaeus § 9), the nature of Euboulides' suit is not clear. Perhaps he attempted to set aside Hagnias' supposed will, so that he could inherit by the law of intestate succession. Or again, by accepting the will he could hope to marry Hagnias' adopted daughter as an *epikleros*. In either case he would be pressing his claim as next of kin. The defendant was apparently one or the other of Hagnias' brothers, since we must alter the reading of the mss., προσκλαίουσα, and πρὸς Γλαύκωνα and πρὸς Γλαῦκον are paleographically likely. Euboulides probably sued him as the girl's guardian. Theopompos implies that Euboulides predeceased the girl, and he has no apparent reason for lying. Therefore, I date Euboulides' suit soon after Hagnias' death c. 396. It is not certain whether suitors had to wait until an heiress reached marriageable age before filing a claim in court.[34] If so, Euboulides

[33] I also think that Stratios, the son of Phanostrate, although a second cousin, would have ranked below the others, if he had not been able to trace his connection to Hagnias through his father as well.

[34] Harrison, I, 138.

may have been seeking a way around this restriction by establishing himself as the girl's guardian, with a view toward marrying her when she did come of age. The law cited at Ps.-Dem. 46.18 says that an heiress' *kyrios* is to marry her. Perhaps, then, Euboulides sued Glaukon or Glaukos to supplant him as guardian. In any event, he failed. Naturally, Sositheos does not dwell on that, but instead uses this testimony to show that Euktemon recognized his nephew's priority, i.e., through the maternal line. (Of course, if getting Hagnias' estate required marrying the girl, perhaps Euktemon simply was not interested.) From this deposition we can see that Euktemon was no longer alive.

44. These witnesses are probably the ones who gave the first evidence in section 36. From them we learn for the first time that Philagros remarried after Phylomache died and had another son, Menestheus. (Only this deposition and the next tell us who he is; Sositheos refers to him in section 74 as a relative of his wife's.) The importance of this testimony is that Menestheus recognizes the priority of his half-brother's claim (through the maternal line) and so the position of the elder Phylomache. I take it that the references to Euboulides' claim in §§ 43-45 all pertain to the same trial.

45. This deposition adds nothing to the previous one. The witness is perhaps identical with the adopted son of Archilochos who testifies at § 37, but this requires emending "Archilochos" to "Archimachos" or *vice versa*.

Broadbent says (102) that "Straton and Archimachos should be witnesses to Menestheus' parentage on behalf of his father's and mother's family respectively." If this were true, they would have done well to establish their credentials with the jury. I doubt that after such a long interval Sositheos could be so choosy about lining up his witnesses.

46. This witness must be either Sositheos' brother or his first cousin, for both he and Sositheos are sons of a daughter of Kallistratos. We know further that Sositheos married his daughter to his nephew. (Cf. 74.) This witness may be the father of that nephew. I think that he also made the second deposition in section 37.[35] Interestingly enough, his mother did not tell him about the

[35] If we are dealing with two witnesses, there are several possibilities for their relationship. If Kallistratos had only one daughter, Sosias must be the witness in 37 and his son (Sositheos' brother) here. If Kallistratos

attitude of their relatives toward Euboulides' suit. Since it appears that Sositheos was born at about the time Hagnias died,[36] his mother and aunt may have been too young to be concerned with Euboulides' litigation at that time.

The depositions. Some scholars, as we have seen, think that some of the witnesses in sections 35-37 reappear in sections 42-46. It is my hypothesis that in fact the two groups of deponents are entirely identical. Sositheos first had them testify succinctly to the main point at issue, that Phylomache was the full sister of Polemon, and then had them add whatever else they knew. Several considerations support this interpretation. In the first place, it would be strange if the first group of witnesses knew Phylomache's ancestry but had nothing further to add in support of Sositheos' case. Secondly, it is manifest that the witnesses in sections 42, 44, 45, and 46 also know that Phylomache is the full sister of Polemon. However, the first deposition completely obscures this point, while it seems to me that the jury could hardly get the full impact of it in sections 44 and 45, where Phylomache's position is mixed in with all the other relationships. Charge Sositheos with bungling, if you will, but if these witnesses are simply repeating and add to what they have already said, the process is far more intelligible. The next thing in favor of my suggestion is its elegance. Consider the source of each deponent's information:

deponent		source	deponent		source
35	plural	themselves	43	plural	themselves
36A	plural	their father	44	plural	their father
36B	singular	his father and others	42	singular	his father
37A	singular	his father and others	45	singular	his father
37B	singular	his mother	46	singular	his mother

This seems to me a very striking coincidence. Before considering the drawbacks of my interpretation, I just add the fact that the father of the witnesses in 44 is Straton, while the grandfather of those who give the first testimony in 36 is Stratonides. Clearly

had two daughters, the two witnesses can still be father and son, connected with one daughter or the other. Finally, one could be the husband of one, the other the son of the second.

[36] He probably married Phylomache c. 370 (cf. *supra*, on Isaeus 9) when he was about thirty. Hagnias died c. 396.

these two names came into the family of the Bouselidai when Oinanthe married into another family which used them. If these two sets of brothers are not identical, they are very closely related. Shall we believe that one set knew only Phylomache's parentage, while the other knew many additional genealogical details?

The first difficulty with my proposal is the matter of self-identification. In all five cases the man (or men) offering the second deposition identifies himself in a completely or slightly different way from the man giving the first deposition. If one will not accept this variation as a matter of personal choice, I can only suggest that the witnesses hoped to add to their credibility by naming additional relatives in their second depositions.[37] In any event, this difficulty argues also against the view that *any* of the depositions involves duplication, as much as it does against my notion that *all* of them do. The second obstacle, which seems to me much more important, is that we require two emendations in the text. Although editors normally reconcile the "Archilochos" at 37 and the "Archimachos" at 45, there is no compelling reason for doing so. Secondly, the second witness at 37 testifies that "the father of his wife, Kallistratos, is a cousin from uncles to Polemon, and his mother is a child of cousin to Polemon," while the deponent at 46 says that "the father of his mother, Kallistratos, is a brother to

[37] Any explanation of why the witnesses identify themselves or their informants as they do is bound to be subjective. To maintain my theory I would have to say that the witnesses at 36A and 37A link themselves only with Polemon in their first deposition because he is Phylomache I's closest relative and they are testifying about her parentage. In their second deposition (44-45), where they discuss family affairs at greater length, they claim kinship with the three branches of the family that are involved in the suit. Other witnesses connect themselves in their initial testimony with the heads of the two families involved in the critical marriage between Phylomache and Philagros, either with the older generation of Polemon and Philagros (35) or with the younger one of Hagnias and Euboulides (36B). In the second round one deposition (43) repeats this identification with the two family heads and adds the name of Euktemon because the testimony is mainly about his attitude. The other witness (42) does not repeat his identification with the younger heads of the two families but instead names only Polemon, who is the point of reference in his deposition: he starts from Polemon and names his cousins, then passes to the relationship among the offspring of these cousins. The fifth witness (37B) first calls Kallistratos a cousin to the most important members of each of the other two branches, Polemon and Charidemos, but in the second deposition (46) he names Kallistratos' two brothers and then says that all three were cousins to Polemon and Charidemos. Actually, then, only this last instance is hard to fathom.

Euktemon . . . and Philagros." I propose to emend the word "wife" to read "mother" to bring the two into agreement: "The father of his *mother*, Kallistratos, is a cousin from uncles to Polemon, and his mother is a child of cousin to Polemon." This, it seems to me, makes much better sense and agrees with Sositheos' use of ἀνεψιοῦ παῖς in a genealogical chain to mean first cousin once removed. A final objection is that section 46 does not really add much to the second deposition in 37. Broadbent, in fact, makes the excellent suggestion (102) that Sositheos held it back from its proper position directly after 37 in order to make it seem independent confirmation and to draw the jury's attention back to the main point, Phylomache's parentage. My version is that the witness really had nothing to add to his previous testimony except for identifying Phylomache's husband, but Sositheos felt that he had to recall all five witnesses (or groups), and this final piece of testimony is, as Broadbent says, a good recapitulation.

The question of the authenticity of these depositions gave rise to a sterile debate among philologists in the nineteenth century.[38] Nothing I have seen proves that they are fakes, but it is perhaps equally difficult to devise a test of their genuineness. If some documents in the speech are genuine, such as the law of Drakon cited at § 57, that still does not preclude the possibility that a forger inserted some of the others. For that very reason, if we reject the chronological deposition at § 31, that is no blow at the status of these genealogical *testimonia*. If we find that these documents agree with the information provided by Theopompos and Sositheos, it simply proves that the hypothetical forger was alert, and if he has invented names not found elsewhere, we have no way to check him.[39] I accept these depositions as genuine on the ground that a forger would not have been clever enough to invent them. To do so, he would have to determine that Euboulides II was related to Hagnias II through his own father *and* mother and then to

[38] Cf. Adolfus Wachholtz, *De litis instrumentis in Demosthenis quae fertur oratione in Macartatum* (Kiel, 1877) and E. Drerup, "Über die bei den Attischen Rednern eingelegten Urkunden," J. f. C. P. Supp. 24 (1898), 325-332.

[39] Some say that the reference in 42 to Phanostrate daughter of Stratios is an indication of forgery since the name should be Phanostratos, but in discussing that section we concluded that Phanostrate is correct. The depositions also specify that Menestheus is the uncle of Phylomache II, but at 74 Sositheos calls him merely a relative.

invent characters who would exemplify this duality. First, he has invented Euktemon to show that someone with a better claim in the paternal line stepped aside because he recognized Euboulides' priority through Phylomache. Then he devised a second marriage for Philagros, so that Euboulides could have a homopatric brother, who like Euktemon would yield to his superior claims in the maternal line. Then he had to invent an occasion for these relatives to yield, *viz.*, Euboulides' suit against Glaukon or Glaukos. And he did all of this without any prompting from the text. In short, the forger has understood the case far better than most modern interpreters.[40]

Most scholars seem to be convinced that Phylomache was the legitimate full sister of Polemon, but I cannot see why. The woman was born almost a century before this trial, so that there really was no way of proving the point one way or the other. Broadbent[41] argues that "doubts about Phylomache's paternity appeared only" after her granddaughter had won Hagnias' estate. But there is a simple explanation for this fact, if indeed it is a fact. Suppose that Hagnias I chose to raise an illegitimate daughter and then got his nephew to marry her. It would be in the interest of both families to pass her off as legitimate, and no outsider could expose her. Even distant relatives like Oinanthe might be deceived. Eventually Phylomache would come to be accepted as Polemon's sister. Then, however, a curious chain of events led to the extinction

[40] If there is a forger, he has added various circumstantial details, such as the adoption of the witness in 37 by his maternal grandfather, Euktemon's term as *basileus*, and, apparently, the very name of the speaker, Sositheos. The name is otherwise mentioned only in the *hypothesis*, which is derived entirely from this speech and incorporates nothing from Isaeus. Probably the best argument against the documents is Sositheos' failure to use them effectively, but that seems characteristic of him. Notice especially how he fails to use the laws which he cites at §§ 57-58. Perhaps he was simply trying to overwhelm his listeners with the *amount* of material he presents. If I am right in saying that the two sets of witnesses are identical, the internal consistency of their testimony is strong support for its genuineness.

[41] *Op. cit.*, 98: "When Phylomache II first claimed and won the estate from Glaukos and Glaukon, it is difficult to believe that Hagnias' mother at that time alleged the non-existence or non-Bouselid paternity of Phylomache I, and indeed Theopompos claims all the credit for exposing the falsity of Phylomache II's genealogy, while Sositheos agrees that the 'great lie' came from Theopompos." Glaukos and Glaukon's concern at the trial was to defend the will, not to defame Phylomache; naturally Theopompos takes all the credit for exposing her, and even more naturally Sositheos avoids mentioning that Hagnias' own mother opposed his side.

of Hagnias' house, and the younger Phylomache obtained possession of his estate and cult. His mother, knowing the truth about the lineage of this woman, was incensed and told her sons and her brother, Stratios. Only then did the truth come out. Hagnias' mother had a strong motive to lie, if necessary, about Phylomache in order to help her sons obtain his property, but she had even stronger motives to tell the truth if that would recover her son's estate and put his cult into the protection of his brothers. The fact of the matter, in my opinion, is that we shall never know the truth about Phylomache's parentage.

47-50. While it may seem to the modern reader that Sositheos does not have enough confidence in the testimony of his own witnesses to base his case on it, we must recognize that Athenian orators preferred to use what Aristotle (*Rhetoric* 1355b) calls "artistic proofs," arguments from probability and the like. Here he resorts to an argument based on names, returning to his basic point that Theopompos and Makartatos are only interested in Hagnias' wealth, while he himself wants to preserve Hagnias' family.

Isaeus himself employs this imaginary examination (ἀνάκρισις) of an opponent at 1.36-37 and 2.25. Sositheos has already effectively used this repetition of the question in section 25. There too we find a *tour de force* of names which helps the jurors keep in mind the genealogical relationships among the Bouselidai.

Actually, the masculine names in Hagnias' family are Hagnias and Polemon, which do not recur among the descendants of the elder Phylomache, including Sositheos' line. Phylomache is the only name that is common to both groups of kin, and that, only if the first Phylomache actually was the daughter of Hagnias I. The argument either is redundant or begs the question. Nevertheless, it must have been effective, for Makartatos later apparently named one of his children after Hagnias.[42]

51. We have already discussed the text and interpretation of the inheritance law. (Cf. the commentary on Isaeus 2.) Suffice it to say that whatever emendations we make, it ought to be clear by now that inheritance devolved on paternal relatives up to and including second cousins before reverting to the maternal kin. Perhaps we need only comment here on the law's application

---

[42] Cf. Reinmuth, *op. cit.*, 58.

to bastards. We find scattered references to decrees passed during the last years of the Peloponnesian War aimed at increasing the population.[43] Athenaeus (556a), for instance, mentions one legalizing bigamy. Whether any of these proposals were actually adopted, there certainly must have been an increase in bastardy during the war. For Thucydides tells us (2.53) that traditional Athenian morality was destroyed as a result of the plague, and this situation can only have been aggravated when the rural population was uprooted from its ancestral home and crowded together into hovels in the city.[44] The opportunity to contract liaisons with foreign women, for instance, was greatly increased, and in the anonymity of the city men could do things they would not have dared to do in their home villages. If the Athenians actually did relax the marriage laws during the war, they tightened them once the emergency had passed.[45] As a result there was a nasty problem of what to do with the numerous bastards born during the war. At the same time the Athenians determined to forgive and forget most of the crimes which they had perpetrated on each other during the civil strife in 411 and 404.[46] They also proclaimed an amnesty for most other previous transgressions and were amazingly faithful in adhering to their resolve. They applied the same standard in dealing with the problem of illegitimacy. Bastards born before 403/2 were allowed to inherit, those born in that year or later were not.[47]

52. The law, in fact, says nothing about "houses", and the meagre treatment Sositheos affords it is to me a strong indication

[43] Cf. Diogenes Laertius 2.26; Athenaeus 556a; Aulus Gellius 15.20; Suidas, s.v. λειπανδρεῖν. Perhaps they all refer to the same enactment; cf. Leonard Woodbury, "Socrates and the Daughter of Aristides," Phoenix 27 (1973), 24-25.

[44] Cf. my article, "An Interpretation of the 'Demotionid' Decrees," Sym. Os. 42 (1967), 60-65.

[45] Aristophon of Azenia moved a law which provided that "whoever is not born of a citizen mother is to be a bastard," while a certain Nikomenes added another that "no one of those (born) after Eukleides became archon [403/2] is to share citizenship, unless he proves both parents citizens, but to let off those (born) before Eukleides without scrutiny." Cf. Athenaeus 577b; the scholion to Aeschines 1.39; Isaeus 8.43; Demosthenes 57.30.

[46] Andocides 1.73-91; *Ath. Pol.* 39-40; cf. also Alfred P. Dorjahn, *Political Forgiveness in Old Athens* (New York, 1946).

[47] At least, that is my interpretation. Possibly, however, if a bastard had not entered an inheritance by 403/2, he could no longer do so. But certainly the law did not deprive him of what he had already inherited. Isaeus quotes this law at 6.47.

that he cannot refute Theopompos' claim. An argument like the preceding one on names would have been devastating. "What is an ἀνεψιοῦ παῖς? Surely the παῖς of one's ἀνεψιός. Who is Hagnias' ἀνεψιός? Who is his son? Who, then, is his ἀνεψιοῦ παῖς?" In contrast, when Theopompos cites the same law at section 11, he shows precisely how it applies to his opponent, sticking to the letter of the law.

53. Having completed his presentation of the depositions and the inheritance law, Sositheos turns from narrow legalities to a loftier and safer topic, the interdependence of rights and responsibilities. In the third section of his proof he will claim that his family has a moral right to the estate since they have honored the deceased. This will be much easier for him to argue and will also provide the jury a better motive than legal quibbles to overturn the previous decision against his wife. (Isaeus himself uses much the same strategy on several occasions; cf. 1.39-47, 4.19-23, and 8.31-32.)

This argument from equity places Makartatos at a great disadvantage, for he cannot even pretend to have done much to merit his inheritance. However, if one looks closely, he will see that Sositheos actually performed no favors for Hagnias, but rather for his own wife and father-in-law. If, in fact, they are Hagnias' legitimate heirs, then, of course, Hagnias' family did benefit from Sositheos' actions. Yet, if Sositheos could prove that, the rest of his speech would be formally redundant.

54. If an *epikleros* belonged to one of the three highest property classes, her inheritance would serve as her dowry, but a poor orphan without brothers would need assistance. If she had relatives of the same rank, say two cousins, there must have been a process to determine which would marry her, although we do not know what it was.[48] If, on the other hand, both wanted to avoid marrying her, they each put up half the dowry. If two sisters had only one cousin, he did not have to dower both. He shared the obligation with the next in line, say a second cousin. This is one of the laws which could be enforced by a member of the general public as well as the victim or his representative. While in most cases an Athenian had to have some personal interest to bring suit, in special circumstances this requirement was not in force.

48 Cf. Andocides 1.117-121.

For instance, in a matter involving the public any citizen was competent to sue, while even in a few private matters it might be necessary for an outsider to intervene. So here the nearest relative would be the heiress' representative in court, and she might require help from someone else to keep him in line. As usual in cases involving the family, the eponymous archon was the magistrate in charge.

55. This is the third time Sositheos has advanced this deceptive argument (cf. §§ 13 and 20), but the first reference to the ages of the two rivals. On our chronology he was born c. 400, while Theopompos was already an adult when Hagnias was killed a few years later. A difference of fifteen years in their ages seems compatible with what Sositheos says here.

56. Examples of the strategy of repetition: by saying it often enough Sositheos might eventually convince the jury that his wife is Hagnias' cousin, and, of course, "shameful" and "polluted" are among his standard terms for the opposition.

57-58. We actually have portions of three separate laws here. The first is Drakon's law on involuntary homicide, as reaffirmed by a commission charged with codifying the laws at the end of the fifth century. Since we also know this law from a badly worn inscription,[49] we can see that Sositheos or a subsequent copyist was very lax in transcribing its provisions. In this inscription the section about making pronouncement comes after the regulations for prosecution and forgiveness. Moreover, in our version an entire line is missing: if there are no fathers or sons alive to forgive the homicide, that power falls to the cousins μέχρ' ἀνεφ[σι]ότετος καὶ [ἀνεφσιõ]. (For the meaning of these kinship terms cf. the commentary on 62.) It is also noteworthy that the mss. list five classes of kin who are to join in prosecution where the inscription has room for only four, and these in a different order. The stone lists cousins first, and the mss. put them third. The stone has no room for ἀνεψιαδοῦς. Presumably, this word crept into the mss. as an explanation of the rare term ἀνεψιῶν παῖδας. (We cannot tell whether the annotator meant ἀνεψιαδοῦς as "first cousins once removed" or "second cousins," as the lexicographer Pollux uses it [3.28].)

For a full discussion of the Athenian homicide law cf. D. M.

[49] See Ronald S. Stroud, *Drakon's Law on Homicide* (Berkeley and Los Angeles, 1968).

MacDowell, *Athenian Homicide Law in the Age of the Orators* (Manchester, 1963). In summary, it provided that the Areopagus try a man accused of murdering a citizen, and the *ephetai* other types of homicide. The *ephetai* were originally chosen according to aristocratic principles but later by lot. Some scholars have concluded that regular juries of several hundred supplanted them during the fourth century, but MacDowell shows that there is no foundation for such a view. (52-56) Of course, in the Athenian system of self-help justice the prosecutors are the victim's relatives, but what is interesting is the requirement that various classes assist the nearest kin. We cannot determine how Drakon used the terms γαμβροί and πενθεροί. For in Attic prose the terms were no longer used, and the dramatists use them indiscriminately. Perhaps Drakon employed them in the sense given by Pollux (3.31), πενθεροί as the bride's family, γαμβροί as the groom's. The penalty for involuntary homicide was automatically exile, but the law permitted the relatives to waive the penalty.[50] Since the kin were acting not so much on their own behalf as on behalf of the deceased, it looks as though they required this express permission in order to overcome their religious scruples or superstitious awe of the victim and become reconciled with his killer. If that is so, then this provision is a milestone on the passage from the savage system of revenge and blood feud arising out of a killing to a system of justice administered by the state. In the rare event that the deceased had no cousins or closer kin, the *ephetai* were to choose ten members of his phratry to decide about forgiveness. This appears to be a survival from archaic times, when selection according to rank was accepted practice.

By way of contrast, the second law is written in the language of the fully developed democracy, with its frequent threats to penalize any magistrate for neglect of duty. Its purpose seems to be to eliminate as quickly as possible any religious pollution which would contaminate a village from the presence of a dead body and to lay the responsibility for payment on those who will inherit the deceased's estate. In the case of a poor man apparently the relatives in general, rather than a single heir, had to pay.

The third law also appears to belong to the late fifth or early

[50] Perhaps this involved payment of blood-money; cf. Robert J. Bonner and Gertrude Smith, *The Administration of Justice from Homer to Aristotle*, II (Chicago, 1938), 192-231.

fourth century, when the Athenian state began to take control of local cults,[51] and the *basileus*, as its chief religious official, assumed responsibility for letting lands belonging to those cults. The best example of this practice is an amendment to a decree passed in 418/7 which authorizes two separate transactions, the sale of mud from the shrine of Neleus and the leasing of the land, presumably after competitive bidding: "the *basileus* and the *poletai* shall let the temenos of Neleus and Basile, according to the provisions of the commissioners, on a lease of twenty years; and the lessee shall enclose the sanctuary of Kodros, Neleus, and Basile at his own cost, and whatever money the temenos yields as its annual rent he shall pay down to the *apodektai* in the ninth prytany; the *apodektai*, in accordance with the law, shall hand it over to the treasurers of the Other Gods. And the *basileus*, or any other person in whose charge these things have been placed, if he shall not do that which has been decreed, during the prytany of Aigeis, shall be fined one thousand drachmai. The person who buys the mud shall remove it from the trench, when he has payed its price to Neleus, during the existence of the present Boule. The *basileus* shall erase (the name of) the buyer of the mud, whenever he shall make the payment, and in its place he shall write upon the wall (the name of) the lessee of the temenos with the amount of the rent and (the names of) the bondsmen, according to the law for the regulation of sanctuaries. For the information of such as desire it, the secretary of the Boule shall cause the decree to be engraved upon a stone stele and shall set it up in the Neleion next the staging, and for this purpose the *kolakretai* shall give the money. The *basileus* shall let the temenos of Neleus and Basile under the following conditions: the lessee shall enclose the sanctuary of Kodros, Neleus, and Basile according to the provisions of the commissioners during the term of the Boule now entering upon its duties, and he shall cultivate the temenos of Neleus and Basile in the following way: he shall set out no less than two hundred young olive trees, and more if he chooses; and the lessee shall have control over the trench and all the rain water which flows within the Dionysion and the gate at which the *mystai* go forth to the sea, and within the public building and the gate which leads to the Bath of Isth-

[51] Cf. my article, "Internal Evidence for the Date of the Kallias Decrees," Sym. Os. 48 (1973), 38-39.

monikos. The lease shall run for twenty years."[52] The Boule's original proposal required the sanctuary to pay the cost of fencing. Presumably this amendment would cause the lessee to offer a lower rent. It may also be that the requirement to plant two hundred olive trees was more stringent than the original terms. At the expiration of the lease the trees must have become the property of the cult.

If the mud merchant or the olive grower failed to pay what he owed, he became a public debtor and, consequently, automatically ἄτιμος, without the necessity of a trial. Athenians recognized various forms of *atimia,* ranging from complete outlawry (meaning that anyone could kill an *atimos* with impunity) to the loss of various civil rights, such as the right to address the assembly.[53] A public debtor lost most other civic rights as well and was banned from the Agora and participation in religious rites. Once such an unfortunate died, his disabilities passed to his descendants. There is some dispute over how this rule was applied. The main problem, it seems to me, is to determine the meaning of the text which Sositheos cites. Surely a man's entire clan was not deprived of rights; instead, γένος means "descendants", "progeny". But by '*their* heirs' does the law mean the heirs of the debtors or the heirs of the progeny? Either seems acceptable Greek to me, and the distinction would have little practical application. In either case *atimia* would pass from heir to heir indefinitely until someone finally paid the debt.[54] While the meaning of the text, then, is generally clear, some scholars have refused to believe that the law could actually mean what it appears to say. According to Harrison (I, 128, n. 2), "as it stands this clause means that, where a man died in debt to a temple, any heir, whether direct descendant or not, was personally liable till the debt was discharged. This throws this type of liability so very much wider than is suggested anywhere else that commentators have tried to water the passage

[52] *I.G.* I², 94. The translation is modeled after that of J. R. Wheeler, "An Attic Decree; the Sanctuary of Kodros," A. J. A. 3 (1887), 39-41.

[53] Cf. Harrison, II, 169-176.

[54] Louis Gernet, "Note sur les parents de Démosthène," R. E. G. 31 (1918), 188, suggests that the phrase "progeny and their heirs" be taken together as referring to a single group, i.e., only descendants who are the heirs. But the choice of words here seems impossibly obscure to express what could be said so much more lucidly by "progeny, if they be heirs," "progeny, whoever is an heir," or "progeny, those being heirs."

down . . . by striking from the text the words καὶ κληρονόμους τοὺς τούτων." In fact, however, this is an extremely weak argument from silence, for while some of the surviving speeches do mention people caught up in their father's or grandfather's *atimia*,[55] there is little *a priori* likelihood that they would involve a nephew or cousin who inherited the disability. After all, Isaeus and the other orators represented those who stood to gain rather than lose by proving their right to inherit. Actually, it would help Sositheos' case much more, if *atimia* passed to collaterals such as his son.

59. It is remarkable that Sositheos makes no attempt to elucidate the laws just read. In fact, if the mss. did not contain them, we would have no idea of what they were. To be charitable one might say that they make his point so clearly that no commentary is needed. On the other hand, these laws are not really applicable in this case. The last two cannot possibly concern Hagnias, and it is inconceivable that Sositheos and his allies had any part in denouncing Hagnias' Spartan murderers, while, if the Spartans returned his bones to Athens for burial, that task fell to his mother and brothers. Since Sositheos cannot show that he actually carried out these duties for the deceased, he must be content with his general proposition that rights and responsibilities go together. Of course, these laws say nothing about "houses".

60-61. For the sake of variety Sositheos interrupts the exposition of his doctrine to rebut one of Makartatos' contentions. In so doing, he makes one of his most effective rhetorical points. Makartatos must have admitted that he and Euboulides' adopted son stood in the same relationship to Hagnias, for Euboulides and Theopompos were his second cousins through their fathers. The reason that he and not his opponent was entitled to the inheritance is that Euboulides predeceased Theopompos, who was finally left as the sole living second cousin. This is the same argument Theopompos himself used against his nephew (§ 10) and is completely justified in law. Once Theopompos had inherited Hagnias' property, it passed to his heirs *regardless* of their own relationship to Hagnias. But Sositheos is right in turn to say that Makartatos must justify Theopompos' claim to the inheritance. That is, after all, what he means by his rhetoric that the contest involves, not the order of deaths, but whether the more distant relatives have driven out the closer.

[55] Demosthenes 22.34, 24.201, and 58.17.

In addition, I would suggest that Makartatos raised the standard complaint that Sositheos had waited so long to bring suit, had in fact delayed until Theopompos would no longer be alive to defend himself (cf. § 67). Sositheos does not bother to cite here the law which permits a challenge up to five years after the death of the victorious claimant. Instead, he goes on the offensive by setting up a straw man and destroying it with sarcasm. The essential characteristic of this technique is to misrepresent what the opposition has said. In this instance Makartatos complained about something *connected with* his father's death (perhaps, as I say, that Sositheos waited until then to bring suit), but Sositheos twists his position to seem that he complained of the death itself, which is obviously easy to ridicule.

62. On the day after death the deceased's body was laid out in his house on a bier of some sort, such as a bed or couch. The next morning it was carried to a cemetery for burial. It was the task of the women to prepare the body: washing, anointing, clothing, decking it with flowers and jewellery. They also engaged in the traditional forms of lamentation, tearing their hair and beating the breast.[56] It is not clear whether unrelated young women were banned from participation in these rites in order to prevent sexual encounters or to avoid pollution of childbearers by contact with death. At any rate, older women enjoyed greater freedom in general than younger ones.[57]

The mss. say that attendance on the deceased was limited to ἀνεψιαδαῖ. However, when Sositheos interprets the law to the jury, he uses the very unusual word ἀνεψιότης, which occurs only in legal texts.[58] Since it would be odd to paraphrase a law by using a rare word in place of a common one, I think that the reverse has occurred. The law actually said μέχρι ἀνεψιότητος; a scribe added a marginal or interlinear gloss (ἀνεψιαδῶν) to explain the text; finally the gloss ousted the true reading. This is the only text we have which defines ἀνεψιότης, so that if it is corrupt we have no way of knowing what the word means. However, if the text is correct as it stands, it has interesting consequences. Since

[56] Cf. Donna C. Kurtz and John Boardman, *Greek Burial Customs* (1971), 142-161.

[57] Cf. Aristophanes *Thesm.*, lines 505-516, and *Eccl.*, lines 528-529; Lysias 1.15; Stobaeus 74.33.

[58] Cf. my article, "Some Attic Kinship Terms," Glotta 48 (1970), 79-81.

one Solonian law (the inheritance law) uses ἀνεψιῶν παῖδες, and another ἀνεψιαδαῖ, it would appear that the two terms are distinct, so that the former would mean second cousin, vindicating Theopompos' claim to Hagnias' estate (unless one argues that the codifiers of the law at the end of the fifth century rewrote one of the archaic laws but let the other stand).

63-64. Of course the whole issue is whether Phylomache was in fact Hagnias' aunt, but it certainly does not hurt Sositheos' case to keep repeating his assertion as a plain fact. Once again he has Makartatos at a disadvantage. Of course, his mother was not entitled to participate in Hagnias' funeral, but except in the case of intermarriage, no collateral heir's wife or mother could do so.[59] But Sositheos ignores this in order to provide yet another instance of rights entailing responsibilities.

65. Sositheos makes it appear that his branch of the family had to bear the entire burden of Hagnias' funeral, but Hagnias' own mother and brothers must have been the chief mourners, if indeed Hagnias did have a burial. One wonders whether they welcomed the elder Phylomache to the rites. In any event, Phylomache II was not old enough to take part, if the chronological deposition at § 31 is accurate.[60] It is noteworthy that Sositheos does not explicitly state that his side actually did bury Hagnias, nor does he produce witnesses to testify that they still tend his cult.

It is also worth noting Sositheos' effective use of the particle ἄρα, which in Attic prose regularly shows that the speaker dissociates himself from what he is about to say. Sometimes it expresses only skepticism; here Sositheos clearly rejects the other side's contention (as he sees it) that it can have the benefits and leave the burdens to others.

In trying to take advantage of the fact that he married a relative while Theopompos did not, Sositheos reverts to his tactic of emphasizing the importance of names. Notice that he styles Makartatos' mother by using two names and a demotic which do not

[59] As far as we can determine, it is possible that Theopompos was not married at the time of Hagnias' death. On our reconstruction of the chronology, Makartatos had a son after 345, which should put his birth well after the death of Hagnias c. 396. Of course, Theopompos' first son may have been much older.

[60] Since it places her acquisition of Hagnias' estate in 361/0, we have actually had to suppose that she was born in the 380's; cf. the commentary on Isaeus 9.

occur in the line of Bouselos. (In 64 he also notes that she belongs to a different tribe.)

66. We do not know what prodigy occasioned the Athenian request to Delphi for advice, nor do we understand the significance of the reference to the Amphiones. Some have suggested that it concerns the cult of Amphion and Zethos near Thebes.[61] They were reckoned sons of Zeus by Antiope and seem to be culture heroes, the former renowned for his musical skill, the latter for his work in agriculture. Since another oracle addresses the Athenians as sons of Erechtheus,[62] he is probably the eponym meant here.

Demosthenes says to the jury in one of his cases, "For surely you know this, that you perform all these choruses and the hymns to the god, not only according to the laws regarding the Dionysia, but also according to the oracles, in all which you will find it given in answer to the city, equally from Delphi and Dodona, to establish choruses according to the ancestral rites and to make the streets steam (κνισᾶν ἀγυιάς) and wear garlands."[63] He then quotes excerpts from some of these responses, including one very similar to ours. Taking Demosthenes and section 66 together, we can surely conclude that the rhetorical handbooks included collections of oracles for speakers to use whenever necessary. When Sositheos' speech writer searched there, he managed to find an oracle which suited his needs. Even though the injunction to relatives is so minor a part of the reply, the solemnity (σεμνότης) of the whole document helps to elevate his case from petty materialism to the higher plane which he has been seeking.

67. Sositheos ends this section of his speech by parrying Makartatos' complaint about the delay with a typically Greek rejoinder.

68. Now that he has established the general principle of rights and responsibilities, Sositheos turns to a comparison of his own familial piety with the indifference displayed by Theopompos and Makartatos. As he nears the end of his speech, he becomes more strident in his denunciation of his foes. His favorite epithets

---

[61] Cf. Pausanias 9.5.3-4 and 9.17.3-5; Apollodorus 3.5.5; Plato *Gorgias* 485E-486D; Stobaeus 56.13.

[62] Demosthenes 21.52.

[63] 21.51-53. Two passages from Aristophanes (*Knights*, line 1320, and *Birds*, line 1233) show that κνισᾶν ἀγυιάς had become a stock phrase. It would especially be appropriate to make offerings in the streets to Apollo of the Ways (*Aguieus*), whose statue stood outside many a door in Athens.

for them are no longer sufficient; they now appear in the superlative. And to the other misdemeanours he adds a new vice, *pleonexia*, always grasping for more, a standard accusation.

69. Once again (as in section 55) Sositheos tries to show that Theopompos' own conduct convicts him. His point is that Theopompos decided to strip the estate of its value because he knew that he would eventually lose control of it. (Presumably in such an event he would have been required to restore the money he received to the estate, but without Sositheos' diligence this alleged misappropriation would have gone unnoticed.) Theopompos must have had ample justification for his actions or he would have been brought to justice. Legalisms aside, Sositheos also uses this incident to show Theopompos' utter lack of regard for Hagnias. Isaeus too (5.11) excoriates one of his opponents for buying his wards' ancestral home and tearing it down to make room for his garden.

70. In another case Isaeus says (3.19), "When we go out upon expected transactions which must occur with witnesses, we are accustomed to take along our nearest kin and closest associates to such transactions, but each of us make bystanders witnesses of unexpected and sudden events." Sositheos has apparently done both, probably taking a group of friends to Araphen, some twenty miles from Athens along the east coast of Attica, and there recruiting an additional number of neighbors who were familiar with Hagnias' farm.[64] The coastal area is a desolate place, which figures in Menander as one of those spots where pirates kidnap unsuspecting citizens.[65] However, the hills inland are covered with olive groves.

71-72. Sositheos attempts now to make his case seem more important by transferring attention from private to public wrongdoing. A prosecution for cutting down olive trees apparently took the form of *phasis*.[66] In certain matters of great importance to the state, such as misappropriation of public property or violations of mining leases,[67] private citizens could denounce (φαίνειν) male-

---

[64] Lysias (7.20-22) mentions the possibility of taking the archons along to witness the destruction of olive trees.

[65] *Sicyonius*, ed. R. Kassel (Berlin, 1965), line 355. The deme Halai mentioned there is much more likely the one on the barren east coast near Araphen than the one on the more populous south coast.

[66] Cf. Harrison, II, 218-221; the other *locus classicus* for the Athenian law on the olive is Lysias 7, but it does very little to clarify the matter.

[67] Pollux 8.47; cf. also Ronald S. Stroud, "An Athenian Law on Silver

factors and be rewarded with half the fine levied in case of conviction. They were required to make a minimal prepayment of court costs, thirty drachmai or less. (cf. Harrison, II, 93) *Phasis* was also available against anyone who engaged in (or financed) grain shipments to any destination other than Athens, for the Athenian *demos* (and Greek states in general) took special pains to assure itself of an adequate supply of food. Thus the restrictions on the cutting of olive trees.

73. As part of his doctrine that rights and responsibilities go together Sositheos now tries to show that he has in fact fulfilled his obligations toward Hagnias. Like his depiction of Theopompos and Makartatos this section too can be classified in Aristotelian terms as a proof based on character.[68]

To recapitulate, Habron and the elder Euboulides were two of Bouselos' five sons. In the next generation Kallistratos and Philagros were sons of Euboulides, but we do not know the name of the daughter of Habron.[69] Kallistratos married this woman's daughter and begot Sositheos' mother.[70]

74. Regardless of any possible connection with Hagnias, the younger Phylomache was the *epikleros* of her father, so that his closest relative could claim her. According to the depositions in sections 42-46, Euboulides II had a brother and two uncles, but they must have been dead or unwilling to marry his daughter when the occasion arose. Sositheos was only his first cousin once removed, as was the man who testifies at 37 and 46.[71] We do not know how it was determined which of the two would marry her.

It was normal, although not invariable, practice to name children after their grandfathers. According to the depositions at 44 and 45,

Coinage," Hesperia 43 (1974), 157-159, for an inscription which prescribes proceeding by *phasis* against those who refuse to accept coin of the realm.

[68] Cf. *Rhetoric* 1356a.

[69] The Oinanthe mentioned in section 36 is the daughter of either Habron or his brother Kleokritos, and on my reconstruction of the stemma the father of Phanostrate was the son of one or the other; cf. on § 42 and Isaeus 8.

[70] There is no full study of cross-generation marriage at Athens, but one can cite the examples of Polemon and his wife in this family (cf. Isaeus 8 and 17), the orator Lysias and his niece (Ps.-Dem. 59.22), and Diodotos and his niece (Lysias 32.4). Menekles was obviously much older than his wife in Isaeus 2 (§§ 3-7), and it would appear that Demosthenes' father was considerably older than his (Dem. 27.4-5).

[71] We have concluded that he was either Sositheos' own brother or his cousin, also a grandson of Kallistratos, Euboulides' paternal uncle; cf. the commentary on 46.

Menestheus was Phylomache's uncle, the homopatric brother of her father. We do not know whether Sositheos' nephew was the son of his brother or sister.

The reason which Sositheos advances for his daughter's marriage to his nephew is disingenuous, to say the least. The connection between his own mother and Hagnias is the same as the relationship between Hagnias and Theopompos,[72] which he constantly impugns, and any possible great-grandchildren of hers would be remote from Hagnias indeed. While he used to speak of "the house of Hagnias," that is no longer possible, since neither his mother nor his father was a descendant of the elder Hagnias. Therefore, he has cleverly switched to "the houses from Bouselos" and "the same stock as Hagnias," i.e., the house of Bouselos. However, by any reasonable standards Sositheos' grandchildren would belong to the house of Sosias, not to the house of Bouselos through Sosias' wife. First cousin marriage of this type is so frequent in Athens that we can dismiss the special motive which Sositheos proclaims.[73] Instead, it would seem that he simply regarded his nephew as a worthy mate and perhaps wanted to gratify his brother (or sister).

75. Cf. *Ath. Pol.* 56.7: the archon "is also concerned for the orphans and the heiresses and the wives who warrant that they are pregnant when the husband has died. And he has power to fine the wrongdoers or to bring them into the dikastery."

This law is of interest in illustrating the circumscribed power of the magistrates under the developed democracy. As Harrison explains it,[74] the archon "is empowered to impose a fine within the limits allowed to him (κατὰ τὸ τέλος) for offences against widows or orphans. If he deems the wrongdoer should pay a greater penalty, he is to cite him to appear before a heliastic court, stating on the citation what penalty he proposes: the court first decides whether the man is guilty, and then fixes the penalty by the process of τίμησις; presumably this means that the defendant puts in his estimate of the appropriate penalty and the court decides between it and that proposed by the archon. This upper limit to the value of the fine which a magistrate could inflict without reference to a court differed for the various magistrates. The only

---

[72] They were both second cousins to the deceased.

[73] Cf. my article, "The Marriage of First Cousins in Athenian Society," Phoenix 21 (1967), 273-282.

[74] II, 4-5.

figure for which we have definite evidence is 50 drachmai for the hieropoioi and the proedroi; but we can conjecture that it was at least as high for more important magistrates." (He notes, however, that some authorities take κατὰ τὸ τέλος to mean that the archon has power to fine the culprit *according to his census classification.*) He adds a salutary warning that we "must distinguish from this right to impose a fine up to a certain value the right enjoyed by certain magistrates to adjudicate without reference to a dikastery cases involving claims of less than a certain value." He also extrapolates from this law and a passage in Aristophanes that the usual period between summons and court appearance was at least five days. In the *Clouds* (1131-1142) Strepsiades is summoned four days before the end of the month to appear on the final day.

76. Once again we must remind ourselves that Sositheos has failed to prove that his wife and child are Hagnias' nearest kin. As for Makartatos' name, consider the fact that Sositheos named two of his children after his wife's relatives. Still, he must have scored with this argument, for Makartatos later named a son after Hagnias.[75]

77. Theopompos tells the jury (49) that his wife persuaded him to have Makartatos posthumously adopted as the son and heir of her brother Makartatos. As we have noted (on sections 10-11), the motive for such adoptions ranges from familial piety to the simple desire to obtain an inheritance. Theopompos was probably motivated by both considerations. When Theopompos' other son died, it became necessary for Makartatos to return to his original family, leaving his own son behind as the heir to Makartatos I. We also find others who did this,[76] and again we must recognize that both sentiment and profit entered in. Makartatos then controlled both estates, as Sositheos says. While Sositheos is able to blacken his opponent's character with his failure to provide a son for Hagnias, we must bear in mind that for any Athenian it was a higher priority to provide an heir for his natural father. If any blame attaches, it belongs to Theopompos, not Makartatos, for choosing to give an heir to his brother-in-law rather than to Hagnias. Yet, if Theopompos or Makartatos had actually attempted to get his son adopted as Hagnias' heir, Sositheos undoubtedly would have opposed him every step of the way.

[75] Cf. Reinmuth, *op. cit.*, 58.

[76] Ps.-Dem. 44, *passim*.

78. The Solonian law, which Sositheos had read out earlier (51), provides that "males and the sons of males are to prevail, if they are from the same (ancestors), even if they are further removed in kinship." It is stretching this principle a bit to say that priority in adoption must be given to male relatives, and what Theopompos did was the very same thing that Sositheos did: he allowed his son to be adopted into his wife's family. Again, Sositheos' own boasted descent from Bouselos is in the maternal line.

79-80. In Sositheos' day it was still a popular mode of burial to inter several coffins in the ground on a rectangular plot surrounded by a wall of mudbrick or stone.[77] Thus, rather than emphasizing the enclosed nature of the tomb of the Bouselidai, he must be emphasizing its size. That is, the essential point is that the tomb was large enough to encompass the entire family of the Bouselidai.

As irrelevant as it may seem to the modern reader, Sositheos must have impressed the jury with this suggestion of a long lasting estrangement of Theopompos' branch from the rest of the Bouselidai. For, let it be said again, his case is not founded on the narrow technicalities of the inheritance law and the dubious proposition that the elder Phylomache was indeed Hagnias' true kin; rather the position is that by his actions he deserves the estate, while the neglect shown by Theopompos and Makartatos disqualifies them altogether. The separate burial place is simply another manifestation of their attitude of indifference.

However, one can doubt that Charidemos abandoned the family plot because of hard feeling toward the rest of the family. It is possible that he left the ancestral home to acquire land of his own in a different region of Attica and decided to establish his own burial ground there. If the Hagnias and Euboulides mentioned here are the sons of Bouselos and not their grandsons of the same name, it will mean that all five sons of Bouselos were buried together along with certain members of the next generation, such as Polemon. Perhaps, then, despite its size the tomb was virtually filled by the time Charidemos died. One point of interest here is that Sositheos let slip a golden opportunity to say that the elder Phylomache was accepted into the family burial plot. Obviously she was not.

In another case Isaeus himself (2.36-37 and 46) stresses the

[77] Cf. Kurtz and Boardman, *op. cit.*, 105-108.

impropriety of leaving a man's house to perish, with no one to carry on his name.

81-84. Now that he has gone through questions of fact and law and has discussed the equity of the case, Sositheos in closing appeals to the jurors' emotions, just as Aristotle recommends.[78] Although most of this peroration is simply a rehash of now familiar themes,[79] he does take up one new point which should appeal to the passions: no longer is he merely defending the boy's rights, no longer is he simply paying homage to the deceased, Hagnias; now he undertakes to represent all the honored dead of the Bouselidai, whom he can summon to his side.

81. In the *Apology* Socrates says (34c) that defendants frequently call their children forth to influence the jury. In this case Sositheos has had the boy by his side throughout and has frequently pointed to him. Now he seeks to draw the jury into active participation in the case by making *them* responsible for him.

82. We have already noted Sositheos' clever handling of the adoption issue (14), making it appear that Makartatos was unwilling to contest the boy's kinship to Hagnias when, in fact, he was merely unable to keep Sositheos from introducing the boy as the adopted son of his natural grandfather. It is quite true that by failing to remove the victim from the altar Makartatos in effect voted for this adoption, but the phraters certainly did not pass on the elder Phylomache's ancestry at this ceremony.

83. The metaphor of the suppliant's branch seems quite striking to us, but it may have been less effective on the jury, for Euripides had already used it in his *Iphigenia at Aulis* (1216-1217), and others may have done so in works now lost.

84. After repeating charges of *hybris* and scorn, Sositheos ends by restating his main theme, the preservation of the house of Hagnias.

The verdict. To quote Broadbent, who is by no means a supporter of Theopompos' claim to the inheritance, "An inscription from Oropos ('Eφ. 'Aρχ. 1918 pp. 73 ff.) recording the individuals in a class of *epheboi* of Leontis, and dated to 324/3, names a Hagnias

[78] *Rhetoric* 1419b; in fact, the whole structure of his presentation corresponds to Aristotle's division (1356a) of speeches into their pragmatic, ethical, and pathetic parts, respectively.

[79] By now μὴ ἐξερημωθήσεται ὁ οἶκος and τὰ μὴ προσήκοντα have become almost slogans. Cf. also Ps.-Dem. 44, where 'desolation of the house' is a main theme.

son of Makartatos of Oion: this person should therefore have been 18 years of age in 326/5 and born in 344/3. The appearance of the name Hagnias in the family of Theopompos is almost certainly due to continued possession of the estate of Hagnias II, which is to say that Sositheos almost certainly lost his case." (62)

Some will blame this verdict on Sositheos' incompetence, and some portions of his case do seem poorly managed. He includes too many relatives and kinship terms, and he fails to show the significance of his depositions and the laws which he cites. In these areas he seems to be trying to win by the quantity of his material rather than its quality. But there are several professional touches in the speech, including the *anakrisis* at 47-49 and his observation in section 60 that, though Theopompos has died, the laws and the law courts live on. Indeed, some of his devices can be found in Isaeus: the pathos about the olive grove and the comparison of degrees of kinship (cf. on §§ 69 and 22 for the parallels.) The surest sign of professionalism is the audacity with which he usurps the role of champion of the deceased. Many Athenian speakers join rights and responsibilities, but it would be difficult to find one who has done so little for the deceased while claiming to have done so much. The reason Sositheos lost, and the reason Glaukon lost, is, I suggest, the same. Certainty prevailed over uncertainty. No one questioned Theopompos' place in the family, remote as it was, but a will brought forth a decade after the testator's death and a claim to collateral kinship originating almost a century earlier raised doubts which the jury simply could not resolve.